Highwaymen, Hangings & Heroes

Richard Blacklee

3P
PUBLISHING

Copyright © 3P Publishing
First published in 2018 in the UK
3P Publishing
C E C, London Road
Corby
NN17 5EU

A catalogue number for this book is available from the British
Library

ISBN 978-1-911559-81-8

Cover design: Marie-Louise O'Neill
Highwayman: Tony Rotherham

This book is dedicated to our granddaughter Amber Rose Blacklee who was born while it was being written.
If Amber asks questions, in the future, about her family's past there will now be somewhere to look for the answers.

Highwaymen, Hangings & Heroes
Hidden history of a Midlands family

Contents

1. Highway Robbery

Wary rabbits scattered as horses approached, their white tails bobbing as they darted left and right into the undergrowth beside the road. Soon they had disappeared into the thistles and white campion, yellow and purple vetches, tall rusty docks and pink spears of willow herb. Frederick Richardson the Oxford carrier allowed himself a wry smile knowing that the poachers in this area had now turned to more lucrative crimes than trapping rabbits. The sight of so many rabbits was perhaps prophetic, although he considered the scene would be appreciated by his newly born daughter Amber Rose in a few years' time when she was grown up enough to come riding with him.

Richardson was young and keen and loved horses and driving. He had been around horses for most of his twenty-four years and was proud to have been chosen to drive the mail coach. Jobs were scarce during the economic decline of the 1780s. He shivered slightly and snuggled down into his greatcoat, his eyes scanning the approaching Whittlebury Forest through the morning mist. Caution was required for this was the area where the former poachers now roamed, seemingly at will, accosting weary travellers as they went about their rightful business or returned from Stow Fair. Soft targets with easy pickings for the hardened former casual farm labourers who had turned to lives of crime.

These local highwaymen had at first tried robbing drovers on the cattle trails which crisscrossed this part of central England. However, the herds and flocks proved too valuable to their owners who employed 'heavies' armed with clubs and flintlock muskets to provide protection for the drovers. These former soldiers were a fearful bunch who were generally well capable of seeing off any highwaymen who crossed their path.

The Northampton bound coach was making good time this morning, the road was dry and the surveyors for the turnpike trust had done a fine job of laying the gently cambered stones. Richardson was confident of maintaining excellent speed approaching eight miles in an hour. The sole passenger was William Cotton, the Banbury reporter and newsman dropping off bundles of papers at coaching inns along the route. The guard and bugler who usually accompanied the coach were incapacitated after a heavy night's drinking and had missed the departure. Richardson felt safe enough; he had his excellent dog sitting beside him.

Passing the Green Man Inn (where Dick Turpin is said to have had a narrow escape from the Bow Street Runners fifty years previously) the coach slowed on the uphill approach to Silverstone village. The four horses were huffing and puffing and emitting fierce streams of condensation through their nostrils. The forest darkened as the vegetation closed in with treetops merging above the track. The lead horses unexpectedly snorted and jerked sideways, sensing trouble ahead. Out of the corner of his eye Richardson saw movement as a tall larch tree came crashing down. Instinctively he hastened his horses and coach lurched forward as the slender tree crashed onto the luggage rack behind the driver's head. 'Lucky the coach is all but empty today,' thought Richardson. 'Any passengers up top would have been swept off the roof.'

Wild figures appeared out of seemingly nowhere. Men dressed in smock frocks with faces blackened and with masks concealing their eyes. 'The Culworth Gang.' thought Richardson recognising their distinctive disguise. 'Now we are in for trouble!'

He urged his mounts as the tree tore free of its grip on the back of the carriage. The road behind became a jumble of branches and leaves and bursting bundles of mail and newspapers. There was no time for Richardson to reach for the blunderbuss secured under the seat; his only thought was the safety of his passenger and himself. Despite Richardson's young age, he possessed a natural ability to act decisively in the face of danger. There was no chance he was stopping to reason with these men or pick up the fallen load, he was desperate to escape.

3

Richardson heard cursing and shouting coming from all around. He made out the words, 'You great oaf, Tyrell! You missed them.' followed shortly afterwards by 'Sorry Bowers, the rope snagged.'

'Bowers,' thought Richardson, 'that's a familiar name. 'This is most definitely the Culworth Gang. William Bowers is a ringleader. There is no stopping me now; I'm off to tell the Constable. There might be a reward for information on the current whereabouts of the gang.'

Once safely clear of the forest, Richardson called the horses to a halt and stepped down to see to the needs of his passenger. Cotton was clearly shaken but unhurt. He was over excited by all the action. When Richardson explained they had just had a close call with the Culworth Gang, William Cotton's eyes lit up at the prospect of a good story. 'There might be money in this for him too he thought.' The 2d Mercury published crime reports in the postscript section on the third page of the newspaper, and there would also be enormous sales potential for half penny sheets aimed at the poor. Reports of a trial and execution, with dying speeches, would sell very well if only the perpetrators could be brought to justice.

For the true story of what subsequently happened to William Bowers and other gang members in the year 1787, please turn to chapters 41 and 41.

2. Introduction

I am sure every family has its fair share of characters. Mine certainly has, although I didn't appreciate how many of them there were until I took over family research duties after my cousin Helen O'Neill's untimely death in 2016.

Interesting stories kept cropping up until it reached the stage where I decided I really must commit something to writing before I forgot much of what I had learned. This book is the result. The Highway Robbery story is a 'taster' I invented, although the characters are based on real people. Their true stories are told in more detail in chapters at the end. The remainder of the book is non-fiction and it is as accurate as I have been able to make it from currently available sources.

The book includes mention of three war heroes who won the Military Cross the third highest award for bravery in the UK. There are stories about the long forgotten Boughton Green Fair, the Northamptonshire Ironstone industry, a local Grand National winner, V1 rockets, a heavy bomber crash, a shipwreck, a drunken doctor, a man who met Hitler, a governor of Singapore, sports stars, a BBC star, a crooked solicitor or two, a village battle, and of course, a real-life Highwayman who went to the gallows in Northampton in 1787.

It is written in the first person in an attempt to make it easier to bring the various family threads together. My surname is Blacklee, my mother's maiden name was Gimson and my paternal grandmother's maiden name was Bowers. This simple explanation covers many of the names mentioned in the book. My relationship to the characters, where it exists, is explained as the stories unfold. The book is written in basically chronological order around the various branches of the family. It may be read straight through from the beginning or alternatively the reader may choose to dip in and out as takes their fancy.

Hopefully this book will inspire others to enquire about their ancestors. The task is getting easier all the time. It is surprising how much information I have found from merely typing a person's name into a computer search engine.

3. The Freak Carriage Accident
Frederick Blacklee, 1853-1891

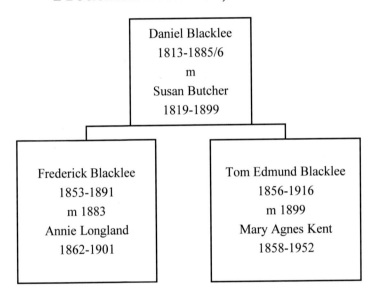

Daniel Blacklee
1813-1885/6
m
Susan Butcher
1819-1899

Frederick Blacklee
1853-1891
m 1883
Annie Longland
1862-1901

Tom Edmund Blacklee
1856-1916
m 1899
Mary Agnes Kent
1858-1952

Frederick Blacklee was born in Wisbech and came to Northampton as a young man with his parents Daniel and Susan Blacklee. Daniel and Frederick were both woollen drapers who established Blacklees Gentleman's Outfitters at Trinity House, 19 Gold Street in the town centre.

19 Gold Street, Northampton in 2018

In 1881, Frederick's brother, Tom, who had been living in Torquay, came to join the family business. Tom was employed as 'cutter and manager of the tailoring department.' His father Daniel assured patrons in a 'letter' that 'Blacklees would execute their commands in as skilful, stylish and punctual a manner as at any establishment in the trade.'

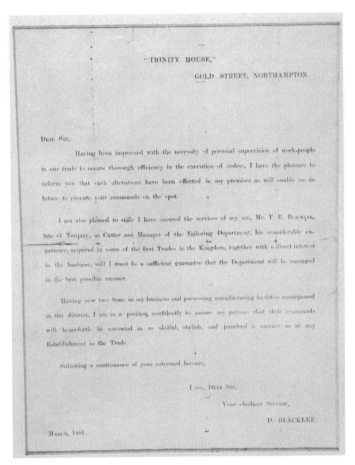

Daniel Blacklee's 1881 letter to customers

In August 1883, when Frederick was thirty, he married twenty-one-year-old Annie Longland at the Union Chapel in Grendon. Annie's family were tenant farmers at The Marquess of Northampton's 250-acre Grendon Manor Farm, where they had farmed for at least a century. It is likely the pair had met through their families' strong religious beliefs.

9

Fred, Bert and Wilf Blacklee in about 1893

Frederick and Annie lived above the shop at 19 Gold Street. They had three sons, Hubert Frederick (Dr Bert), Charles Wilfred (my grandfather Wilf), and Frederick (Dr Fred).

Frederick Blacklee, 1853-1891

Tragedy struck the young Blacklee family at around 8pm on Thursday, 12th March 1891. There was a serious road accident close to Castle Railway Station in Northampton. A report in the Northampton Daily Reporter of 14th March 1891 described what happened:

'Fred was walking past St Peter's Church on Mare Fair, on his way to St James End to see Mrs Friday, when Thomas Thompson of Duston Mills stopped and offered him a lift in his four-wheel dog cart. Fred jumped up and sat in the front with Thomas, with Charles Hedges, a boy working for Thomas, sitting in the back. Just as they got over the West Bridge the trains startled the horse, which pricked up its ears and started off. A tram was standing in front of them near the tan-yard. Fred stood up and jumped out towards the tail of the trap. The horse galloped on and collided with a hand truck. Fred landed on his feet but fell back on to his head. He was taken to Northampton Infirmary at 8.30pm with a fractured skull. He died at half-past four on the Friday (13th) morning. He was just thirty-seven, and left his widow, Annie, with three children whose ages ranged from seven years to only ten days.'

The inquest was held on the Friday afternoon and returned a verdict of accidental death, the verdict being; 'The deceased's death was caused by circumstances over which no man could have had any control.' The newspaper article included a 'memoir,' reporting: 'Fred was a deeply religious man, a junior deacon of College Street Church and a principal mainstay of the YMCA. He was an able speaker, well above the average, and his sermons were always marked by conspicuous merit.'

Four-wheel dog cart. Dogs carried in the box.

I have been unable to find much information about Annie and the children after the accident. At the time of the 1891 census, Annie was residing at Number 7, York Road, Northampton with her mother-in-law, Susan Blacklee, and Susan's sister Sarah Butcher. Frederick's father Daniel, who had founded the business in Northampton, had died around 1885/6.

My great grandmother Annie Blacklee (née Longland) died ten years later in 1901, at the age of thirty-eight. Frederick and Annie are probably both buried at Billing Road Cemetery in Northampton. There is a large gap in headstones along the Barry Road side of the cemetery where a bomb or bombs exploded during the Second World War (see chapter 14). Most likely any family headstones were destroyed.

4. Cads on Castors
Tom Blacklee, 1856-1916

Cads on castors . . .

Members of the Northampton Victoria Cycling Club with their Pennyfarthings

Tom Blacklee came north from Torquay to join his father Daniel and brother Frederick in the family draper's business in Northampton in 1881.

Tom was honorary secretary of the Northampton Victoria Cycling Club. He designed and made their riding uniform, which consisted of thick navy-blue serge suits with knee breeches, high buttoned necks and six buttons down the single-breasted front. Blue caps trimmed with gold braid with the silver club badge on the front, and chamois leather gloves and a police whistle.

The 'Cads on Castors' as they were known must have made a very fine spectacle riding their Ordinary Bicycles (Pennyfarthings) on a group ride accompanied by buglers front and rear! The Victoria Cycling Club met at the Royal Hotel in Gold Street until the 1990s. The hotel was later renamed The Grand and is now a Travelodge.

Tom Blacklee married Mary Agnes Kent at Wantage Parish Church in 1879 and they had five children. Mary's father Alfred was the founder of Kent and Sons furnishings and ironmongers in Market Place, Wantage. Her brother Ernest Albert Kent, a brilliant scholar, went to South Africa in 1898 in the hope the clear air would cure his tuberculosis. He was caught up in the siege of Kimberley during the Boer War and, after returning home, he died in Wantage at the age of thirty-four.

After Tom Blacklee's death in 1916, his son Alf ran the family draper's business in Gold Street, with assistance from his sister Gertie when the shop was busy. Alf smoked like a chimney. He had quite a temper and certainly didn't suffer fools gladly. During the war he was a special constable. Alf died alone whilst on holiday in Folkstone in 1963 aged seventy-seven.

In 1924, Mary Agnes Blacklee commissioned local builders Hawtin to build a large family house for herself and her grown up yet unmarried children Alf, Gertie and Elsie. Elsie taught at a Froebel Kindergarten. Friedrich Froebel was a German educationist born in 1782 who reformed educational methods and teacher training, emphasising development of the whole person/child His philosophy consisted of four basic components: free self-activity, creativity, social participation and motor expression. After my cousin Helen Margaret Smith (Helen O'Neill) was born in 1952 (chapter 39), Gertie wrote to her goddaughter Molly (Helen's mother) expressing delight at the chosen names. She said her sister Elsie 'is awfully pleased you have (another) daughter. She thinks a team of two of the same sex is very nice'.

After Mary Agnes' death in 1952 Kenton was sold and the children moved to their own houses in Weston Favell Northampton.

Kenton, 104 Harlestone Road, Dallington,
Northampton 2018

5. Ironmonger to Doctor
Dr Bert Blacklee, 1884–1961 (the man who left all his money to his girlfriend)

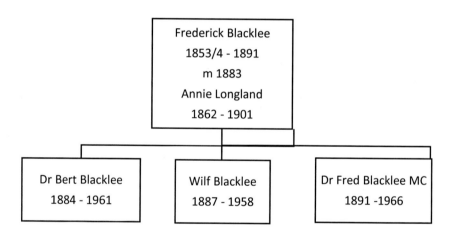

Hubert Frederick Blacklee (Dr Bert) was born in Northampton in 1884. He was the eldest son of Frederick and Annie Blacklee who both died in their thirties.

From what I can gather from scraps of paper in my cousin Helen's notes, Bert, the seven-year-old at the time of his father's accident in 1891, was looked after by the Ashby family. The Ashby connection appears to be from Daniel and Susan Blacklee's third child (of five) Rebecca, born in 1850. Rebecca married a John Ashby from Long Buckby. Another note says, 'Bert went to the Longlands in Northampton.' That may refer to the then twenty-nine-year-old grocer Gersham Longland of 43 Bridge Street Northampton. What I do know for certain is that after his mother Annie's death in 1901 Bert, by then seventeen, went to live at Grendon Manor Farm with the Longlands.

An undated newspaper cutting provides interesting information about Bert after he qualified as a doctor: 'For several years he (Bert) worked for Messrs Johnson and Wright ironmongers in Northampton but left the town to join a similar business in Poole near Bournemouth. While at Bournemouth he was attracted by the medical profession and after having studied for five years at the University of Edinburgh has earned the degrees of M.B. and Ch.B. Mr Blacklee has now secured the appointment of senior surgeon at the Royal Albert Dock Hospital London.'

Bert had already qualified as a doctor when in 1913, aged twenty-nine, he married twenty-one-year-old Mary Hall (May) Timms. May was the daughter of well-known Baptist parents Mr and Mrs Richard Timms of Abbotsford, Abington Park, Northampton. May had attended Castle Hall School Abington Avenue around the same time as my grandmother Olive Bowers (chapter

7). May was editor of the yearly school magazine. She came from 'a big, very wealthy family in Northampton (iron ore barons), a highly respected family.' Her father Richard Timms had been manager of Attenborough & Co's Brixworth Ironstone Co Ltd before being taken into partnership in 1899, the firm subsequently becoming Attenborough & Timms. When Richard Attenborough died in May 1901, Richard Timms assumed control of the business and became the landowner. A fellow leading Baptist, Charles Barlow, was brought in as contractor to do the actual quarrying. Timms occupied offices in George Row Northampton and also managed other quarries owned by the firm. Richard Timms was described as 'venerable looking and bearded.' He was Deacon of College St Baptist Church in Northampton and would have known the Blacklee family for many years.

In 1908, Richard Timms negotiated the sale of the Brixworth quarries comprising tramway, subway, locomotive, trolleys and other plant including 200 wagons to Brixworth Ironstone Co Ltd.

Bert's wedding to May Timms was held at College Street, Baptist Church, Northampton at 9am in 1913 (exact date unknown). Bert's father Frederick (who was killed in the carriage accident in 1891 - chapter 3) had been junior Deacon at this same Church. The early hour of the nuptials was to enable the couple to travel to Scotland the same day to begin their honeymoon.

From left standing: Unidentified man, Gertie Blacklee (29), Elsie Blacklee (22), Miss Timms (black hat), Alf Blacklee (27 - Best Man), Ernest Blacklee (Groom, 29), Bride (21), Wilf Blacklee (25), Olive Bowers (23), JH Longland (53), and Fred Blacklee (22).

Sitting: Mr and Mrs Richard Timms, Polly Morriss (49 - neé Longland), Tom (57) & Agnes (55) Blacklee.

Amongst the presents listed in the newspaper article recording the happy occasion Mr W Blacklee and Miss O Bowers (chapter 7) gave silver tea knives, Mr and Mrs Morriss (chapter 7) some fish knives and Mr JH Longland (chapter 26) a silver tea caddy.

Dr Bert was described as 'partner in one of the oldest and most extensive doctor's practices in Barrow in Furness.' As a doctor he was exempt from military service and spent both world wars at Barrow. He was grandmaster of Lancashire's masons.

Dr Bert retired to Llandudno in 1950 as he 'wanted nothing to do with the nationalisation of the health service under the Labour Government.' He thought his method of charging patients however much he thought they should pay, or could afford, was much fairer! Bert had kept a girlfriend in Llandudno for many years. He took my father Phil to see her and her mother sometimes and Phil recollects that Bert and he always stayed 'at a very posh hotel.'

Bert and May had a house built in Llandudno, Brookside, Abbey Road, which is still there today. It is located close to the seafront at the foot of The Great Orme headland, a massive chunk of limestone rising 200m straight out of the sea. Coincidentally, Bert and May's address in Barrow had also been 'Abbey Road'. Their house in Barrow was called 'Dallington' after their Northampton connection. Nowadays the building is used for offices, until recently occupied by the NSPCC.

Dr Bert Blacklee was born in 1884, and died in 1961, aged seventy-six. Dr Malcolm Blacklee of Pickering remembers him as 'very upright, a dry old stick.' Dr Bert and May had no children. He reputedly left all his money to his girlfriend. His Austin Cambridge car was inherited by his brother Dr Fred.

May died in 1967, aged seventy-five, whilst still living at Brookside.

Brookside, Abbey Road, Llandudno in 2018

Great Orme (centre) viewed from Anglesey

6. First Military Cross
2nd Lt Fred Blacklee, 1891-1966

The youngest of the three Blacklee boys who lost their father in the 1891 carriage accident (chapter 3) was ten-day old Frederick Jnr (Dr Fred). It is likely he was taken by his mother Annie to live with his paternal grandmother Susan Blacklee at York Rd Northampton. He, like his brother Bert may also have lived for a while with their uncle, Gersham Longland, who had a high-class grocery shop in Bridge St Northampton.' Gersham was married but had no children of his own.

After mother Annie's death in 1901, Fred joined his brothers at their maternal grandmother Jane Longland's farm at Grendon. When Fred attended Jane's funeral in 1913, at the age of twenty-two, his address was recorded as 'Rugby.'

Fred is remembered as a great sportsman, particularly as a very good footballer. In the Great War (1914 – 1918) he served with the Territorials. The London Gazette for 14th July 1917 records, under the heading

'Territorial Force – Yeomanry' - 'Cadet Frederick Blacklee to be 2nd Lt 29th June 1917.'

A citation in the Edinburgh Gazette on 11th December 1919 describes the events for which he was awarded the Military Cross, the third level military decoration awarded to officers and other ranks of the British Armed Forces.

'2nd Lt Frederick Blacklee, Royal Wiltshire Yeomanry, machine gunner corps. At Dadizeele during the operations from the 9th to the 14th October 1918 he carried out harassing fire, frequently having to move his guns owing to the severity of enemy shell fire, but continued from his new positions. On the 25th October, 1918, in the Lys sector, he moved forward with the infantry and took up positions guarding the left flank of the brigade, showing great resource. He has shown consistent courage and initiative.'

This must have been one of the final actions of the Great War before Armistice Day on 11th November 1918.

Fred returned to live with his grandparents, the Longlands, in Grendon after the war. His elder brother Wilf had moved to Moat Farm, Whiston after his marriage to Olive Bowers in 1914. Fred was named sole beneficiary under JH Longland's will dated the second of August 1919, after small legacies to Wilf Blacklee, and two employees of the farm, John Capel, and his sister.

1917, Western Front

Dr Fred Blacklee MC and his Great War medals. From left:
Military Cross, 1914 Star, The British War Medal and the Victory
Medal. The latter three are affectionately known together as Pip,
Squeak and Wilfred.

Intriguingly, records show that Fred had asked JH Longland's solicitor to revise the will shortly before JH's death, specifically excluding Fred's brother Dr Bert from any inheritance. The reason stated in the revised draft will, which I believe wasn't signed before JH died, was: 'as he (Dr Bert) is at the present time as far as I can ascertain well provided for by his success in his profession.' It is not recorded whether Dr Bert was aware his brother had gone to such lengths to specifically exclude him from any possible claim over his uncle's estate. Perhaps not, as it was Bert who sponsored Fred through medical school in the 1920s.

Fred Blacklee had hoped to take over the tenancy of Grendon Manor farm after JH Longland's death in 1920. The estate office told my father that the Marquess of Northampton thwarted Fred's plans by refusing him the tenancy. This may have been due to Fred's post-war reputation as a drinker, possibly brought about by a condition which would today no doubt be recognised as PTSD. Rumour has it that Fred was 'frequently merry' and would conceal a bottle of gin in the garden shed when he was staying with his (tee total) brother Dr Bert.

In February 1934 at the age of forty-three, Dr Fred married fifty-seven-year-old Ethel (Mary) Griffiths, the daughter of Alderman TP Griffiths of Southport Lancashire, where Fred was in practice. The ceremony was held at Kensington Chapel London. The couple moved to Bishop's Lydeard in Somerset when Frederick took over the practice of a retiring GP, Dr Frossard. In

1935 they had a property built in Minehead Road, Bishops Lydeard, which they called Grendon House. The impressive looking house is still standing today.

An undated newspaper article describes an incident in which Dr Fred pleaded guilty at Bishop's Lydeard Sessions to driving his car in a dangerous manner on the Taunton to Minehead road at East Combe, on October 24th (year not mentioned). It was 6.55pm, half an hour after lighting up time when Dr Fred was driving a borrowed car on side lights and collided with an unlit stationary tractor and trailer. He was fined £5 with £5 9s costs and had his licence endorsed. On another occasion Dr Fred was in trouble for driving straight across a large roundabout in the centre of Taunton.

Mary died at Bishop's Lydeard in 1940 aged sixty-three after a short illness. Fred was described in the local newspaper's article reporting his wife's death as 'Bishop's Lydeard's much esteemed medical practitioner.' After her funeral Mary was taken back to Southport for burial. Dr Fred and Mary had no children.

Dr Fred Blacklee MC retired to Priory Lane Penwortham Nr Preston and died on 27th February 1966.

7. Pre-war Life on the Farm
The Blacklees

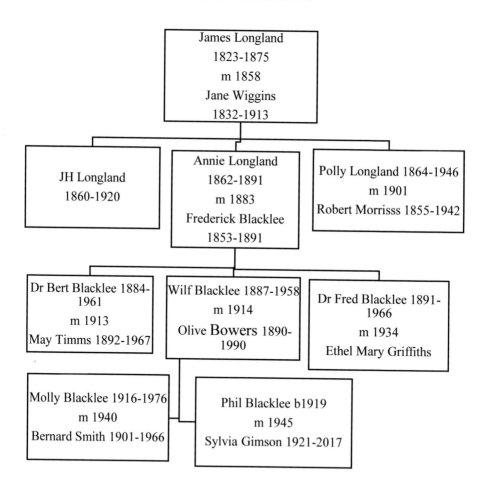

James Longland
1823-1875
m 1858
Jane Wiggins
1832-1913

JH Longland
1860-1920

Annie Longland
1862-1891
m 1883
Frederick Blacklee
1853-1891

Polly Longland 1864-1946
m 1901
Robert Morrisss 1855-1942

Dr Bert Blacklee 1884-1961
m 1913
May Timms 1892-1967

Wilf Blacklee 1887-1958
m 1914
Olive Bowers 1890-1990

Dr Fred Blacklee 1891-1966
m 1934
Ethel Mary Griffiths

Molly Blacklee 1916-1976
m 1940
Bernard Smith 1901-1966

Phil Blacklee b1919
m 1945
Sylvia Gimson 1921-2017

Frederick and Annie Blacklee's middle son, Wilf, (four years old) was cared for following his father's accident in 1891 by Annie's mother Jane Longland at Grendon Manor Farm. Jane's two other children, thirty-one-year-old JH and twenty-seven-year-old Polly were still living at home at the time. By then, the tenancy of the Marquess of Northampton's farm had been transferred to Longland after the death of his father James in 1875 at the age of fifty-two, and a transitional period under trustees. Polly Longland married Robert Morriss in September 1901 and they lived at Waterfall Farm, Chase Park Road, Yardley Hastings.

Wilf Blacklee attended Sibford School near Banbury between the ages of thirteen and fifteen (1900–1902). Sibford School was founded in 1842 as a co-educational boarding school for the children of 'disowned' Quakers – those who had married outside the Society of Friends. It later accepted children from practising Quaker families. The school was based in Walford Manor in the centre of Sibford Ferris, which had been remodelled in the 17th century. It occupied eighteen acres of land and had a strong agricultural bias. The boys worked part time on the farm while the girls did household duties. In this way it was possible to reduce fees to parents, which were adjusted according to means. The school is still going today, and notable recent former pupils include Charley Boorman the TV presenter and travel writer, and Guy Ritchie the film director/producer and former husband of Madonna. Wilf's younger brother Fred also attended the school between the ages of ten and twelve (1901–1903). Also attending Sibford at the same time (1901) was a Lesley Wiggins from Northampton, who was possibly a cousin – due to Polly Longland's mother's maiden name being Jane Wiggins.

Wilf was a border at Sibford School when his mother Annie Blacklee died in 1901 aged thirty-eight. He left school at fifteen to work on his uncle's farm in Grendon. Wilf Blacklee probably met his future wife Olive when RT Bowers moved his family to Grendon House farm in 1898 (chapter 31). Wilf would have been eleven when Olive was eight. They subsequently fell in love and married in St Mary's Church, Grendon, four years later, on 3rd June 1914. A contemporary newspaper article describes the couple as both being 'very popular in the village particularly as the groom held various offices including chairmanship of the parish council and treasurer of the fete committee.' The reception was held at Grendon House and afterwards the couple motored to Northampton, en route to Llandudno for their honeymoon. The best man was the groom's brother Mr F Blacklee (Dr Fred), and the bridesmaids were two of the bride's sisters, Gladys and Rene Bowers.

Initially, the couple settled into Moat Farm, Whiston. The notice of assessment of annual value of property for the year ended 5th April 1923, addressed to Mr CW Blacklee, describes the property as 'house, buildings, land (251 acres) and two cottages.' The owner of the freehold at that time is recorded as Mr Wassell. See chapter 10 for Wassell's connection with the ironstone industry.

Moat Farm, Whiston in 2018

St Mary the Virgin Church, Whiston, 2018

Wilf Blacklee, possibly on his
Brafield-on-the Green farm

Wilf and Olive at Molly and Bernard's wedding in 1940

Wilf and Olive Blacklee's two children were born at Whiston, Maud Mary (Molly), born 29th March 1916, and my father Frederick Phillips (Phil), born 13th November 1919. The excitement of the marriage in 1914, and birth of their first child in 1916, was tempered by the tragic death of Olive's younger brother Doug Bowers fighting the Germans in the Great War in France in October 1915 (chapter 36). A letter from a friend called Dora in May 1916 congratulated Olive on the birth of her daughter and also commiserated with her over the death of Doug. Dora wrote; 'I remember thinking what a nice bright laddie he looked at your wedding, and I know how fond of each other you were.' Dora enquired whether Olive had a good maid to help her with the baby!

Initially, Wilf and Olive travelled locally either by foot, by pony and trap, or by bicycle. When venturing further afield they would catch a bus or take the train. In 1924, Wilf somehow persuaded Olive he needed to buy a four-seater car to take Molly, Phil and their little friend Cath Pain from Whiston Hall to the British Empire Exhibition at Wembley Park. Even at the age of ninety-eight, Phil can recall the excitement surrounding the outing when he was about five. The car was 'black, large and open topped, probably a Rover or something like that.' The 1920s were the great days of steam and the Flying Scotsman engine was one of the highlights of the exhibition. Of the fifty-eight territories which comprised the British Empire at the time, fifty-six participated with displays and pavilions. A 'great national sports ground', called the Empire Stadium, was built for the Exhibition, this later became Wembley Stadium. Around 1926, Wilf and Olive moved to a smaller farm, 'probably about thirty to fifty acres' according to my father Phil, at nearby Brafield-on-the-Green.

Only known picture of Furze Farmhouse

Furze Farm buildings, Brafield-on-the-Green, in 2018

The name of the Brafield farm is spelt in various ways on farming receipts, phone bills etc. my cousin Helen (chapter 39) had saved in her files, including The Furze Brafield, The Furage Piddington, The Firs Piddington, and The Furze Piddington Billing. The postman must have had a hard time delivering the mail! The phone number was Hackleton 22. I believe the correct address is 'Furze Farm' as shown on current OS maps a mile south of Brafied-on-the-Green and close to three spinneys known as High Covert, The Oaks and Ash Spinney. The farmhouse has been demolished and replaced by a modern tractor shed, but the stone outbuildings and the original walled yard are intact and used for timber storage. This is a tranquil rural setting and well worth a visit. In spring time when the horse chestnut trees by the duck pond are in full blossom, the location is quite spectacular. Public footpaths from both Brafield and Denton skirt the farm buildings and join Horton Road near to the Brafield Sports Stadium which is used for stock car racing. Immediately north of the farmstead is a large flat field which used to be a satellite airfield for Sywell aerodrome and both were used for pilot training. This fact was not lost on the enemy and a German spy who was parachuted in to reconnoitre the area was captured nearby during the Second World War. The Yardley Chase army camp and former munitions store is a mile away to the east.

Johnson's Garage Brafield-on-the-Green (known as Johnson & Green in the 1920s) advertised a wide range of goods and services: 'all kinds of repairs to cycles promptly executed, also repairs to gramophones. Wireless of every description. Accessories of all kinds stocked. Sweets and tobacco. Methylated spirits, Primus & Valor cooking stoves and parts, Sun & Hercules cycles, any make of motor cycle supplied, prams re-tyred oil, petrol.' They also advertised as the 'Elson Cycle Works.'

I love the following anecdote; I believe originating from Banbury but which could equally apply to Brafield, of a coaching inn displaying a sign 'Garage & Petrol' at the advent of motor cars around 1900. A local farmer reputedly enquired at the bar the whereabouts of 'the new proprietors!'

Another local business where the Blackees had an account was AW Luck, Shoeing and General Smith and

Wheelwright at Little Houghton. There is an invoice from Luck dated 30 March, 1932 for repairs to a cart and a plough, and for shoeing horses. The farm purchased animal feedstuffs from JJ Wiggins & Son of Harrold. It is quite possible Jane Wiggins (1832–1913) is connected with this business as it is an unusual name. Jane married James Longland in 1858 and was Wilf Blacklee's grandmother. As mentioned above, Wilf was at Sibford School at the same time as a Lesley Wiggins.

Farms were largely reliant on the railway for transporting animal feedstuffs and harvested crops comprising mainly wheat, barley and oats. There were train stations conveniently located within a couple of miles of both the Whiston and Brafield farms at Billing, Castle Ashby and Earls Barton. These stations served the Northampton to Peterborough branch of the London and North Western Railway. On file there is a London Midland and Scottish Railway Company invoice to CW Blacklee dated April 1932 for 'sack charges.' In those days, cereal from the annual harvest would be sent to buyers in two and a quarter hundredweight sacks rented from the railway company. It was possibly transported only a few miles to Whitworth flour mills in Wellingborough, although Phil recollects Liverpool was another regular destination. The name of the 'consignee' on the invoice is Bowers and the bill of £5 13s 2d was paid by Mr RT Bowers. From this it would appear the Blacklees and Bowers farmed closely together. Phil says that as his father was a very poor farmer it was quite likely he asked his father in law Mr Bowers to pay the bill!

Fordson Model F tractor at harvest time

Around 1939, Wilf and Olive Blacklee bought a small farm of their own, with a pretty 18th century stone and thatch house, buildings, with around forty acres. This was Maryland Farm at Number 2, Main Road, Grendon. Phil cannot remember where the money came from to buy the farm; he thinks it may have been a loan from Wilf's older and successful brother Dr Bert Blacklee. Phil says they wouldn't have had to pay very much for a small farm in those days. Neither can Phil remember who previously owned Maryland Farm, although I have established from rating records the name of one former occupier was a Mr Albin Ginns.

The post war period is continued in chapter 25.

8. Boughton Green Fair
1351-1916

My grandmother Olive Bowers' diary entry in June 1910 (chapter 34), 'went to show,' may refer to the famous Boughton Green Fair – the oldest and once the biggest Fair in the Midlands. It was held each year for 600 years under Royal Charter over three days in June, until eventually coming to an end during the years of the Great War of 1914-18.

Boughton Green lies between the villages of Boughton and Moulton on the edge of what has become the Moulton Park Industrial Estate on the northern outskirts of Northampton. Fortunately, the Green itself has been largely preserved from development. As a local boy growing up I heard many stories and rumours about 'goings on' at the Fair, and detectorists still dig up metal coins and artefacts occasionally. The Green is intersected by busy roads and I doubt whether many people passing by are aware of the importance of the site and the ghostly ruins of the former St John the Baptist church.

Immense trade was done in farm equipment at Boughton Green Fair including tools and implements, hurdles and hutches, gates and ladders, troughs and mangers etc. Kitchen ware, cakes and sweets were popular with the ladies and children, whilst sports and sideshows helped attract country folk and vagabonds alike from Northamptonshire and far beyond. The noisiest and most crowded of the three days was usually the last when horses and cattle, including ponies driven from as far away as Dartmoor, Wales or Ireland changed hands. In its heyday, the dust on the roads and showground could be a foot deep! In those early days the event attracted all and sundry from the wealthiest in the land with their fine carriages who came to socialise with their peers, down to common folk bemused by the strange sights, the sounds and the smells: for this was no ordinary country fair. There were exotic birds, animals and reptiles on show. Weird distorted human beings to gawk at, with garish pictures of the fattest, the thinnest, the tallest the shortest, the humpbacked the crippled, displayed outside booths to tempt in voyeurs for a small fee. There were photographic booths and cock fighting, bare knuckle fights, strength competitions and shooting galleries, and to oil the wheels of enjoyment, numerous beer and food booths.

Attendance at the show dropped off towards the end of the 19th century, with traders often complaining of high rents and poor sales. Crime was always a considerable problem with organised gangs particularly from London robbing booths and pick pocketing the gentry and bumpkins alike. The unwary were fleeced with gambling games, the Londoners usually winning any resultant fights. The influx of 'foreign' gangs was so serious by the 1880s that the constabulary called in officers from the Bow Street Runners to help identify the ringleaders. There were assaults and robberies, rapes, and even murders. A farmer from Earls Barton, Joseph Warren, died in 1850 after the accomplices of a gypsy girl he unwisely took off into the woods set upon him. Warren's attackers escaped although Northampton Assizes were always kept busy after Fair week. The death penalty was handed down on numerous occasions although invariably prisoners were reprieved at the last moment and the sentences reduced to severe horse whipping in public. The most notorious incident of public disorder, which did result in a hanging, occurred in 1826. The story of 'Captain Slash' is told in chapter 41.

The great and the good continued to frequent the Fair at least until the end of the 19th century. In 1894, Mrs Jones of the Northampton based Crockett & Jones shoe manufacturing family was injured by a runaway horse. The following year a young horse brought to the Fair to sell by Thomas Bates of Grendon caused the death of a prospective buyer who fell from its back when the horse was spooked by the noisy crowd and reared.

The mood for such Fairs dwindled until it was time to call a halt to the festivities when the country entered war mode in the early 19th century. The landowner Captain Vyse applied to the Secretary of State under The Fairs Act 1871 to have the annual fair abolished. The final fair was held in 1916 and the site was then used by the military for practising digging trenches.

9. King John Connection

Newlyweds Wilf and Olive Blacklee (my grandparents) moved to Moat Farm after their marriage in 1914. I often wondered where the name 'Moat' came from and believe I have recently worked it out; legend has it that King John (1166–1216) had property in Whiston. The remains of earth works are clearly visible in the field between Moat Farm House and Whiston Hall, viewed from the churchyard, and are perhaps the remains of a moat which surrounded an important 13th century residence. Not much is known of King John's early life or loves, other than he was 'sinfully lustful and lacking in piety' and fathered at least five children with mistresses, many of whom were married.

King John died of dysentery in 1216 at Newark during the time of the wars with feuding barons and the French. He upset the Barons by reneging on the Magna Carta agreement he had made with them a year after signing it in 1215. He left a nine-year-old son who was crowned Henry 111. Henry was still fighting the barons in 1264 when he besieged and captured nearby Northampton Castle. In those days, Northampton wasn't the sad town it is today - it was once the third most important town in the land.

Moat Farm, Whiston, 2018

Olive Blacklee with Molly and Phil about 1920

10. Ironstone Quarry
1900–1920s

It must have been very frustrating for Wilf and Olive Blacklee, coming from successful farming backgrounds in Grendon, having to endure the hardships of farming through the Great War years and the 1920s which followed. Wilf always maintained in later life that 'it was the quarrying at Whiston which ruined him', although I suspect the state of the economy had a lot to do with it.

Moat Farm, Whiston was effectively split in two during the Blacklee's tenure by essential ironstone quarrying for the war effort. The hillside south of Cogenhoe Road was excavated with a 600-yard-length north-south face with 40ft deep pit. The ore was transported down the hillside to the LNWR by a specially constructed standard gauge rail track. Phil Blacklee remembers stories of 'great mountains' of ore close to Castle Ashby and Earls Barton Station from where it could be loaded into goods wagons on the LNWR Rugby to Peterborough line. There was also an overhead conveyor bringing iron ore to the tipping station from other quarries north of the river at Earls Barton. The quarry owners were unable to lay rail tracks to these quarries to the north as the river Nene frequently overflowed and flooded the land.

Whiston Quarries had four proprietors during a short working life of less than ten years. Opened by JW (Will) Pain of Whiston Hall in 1914, it was served by a mile-long standard gauge (4ft. 8½) rail line from the LNWR at Cogenhoe Sidings to the west of Castle Ashby & Earls Barton Station. The overburden (which ranged in depth from 5ft at the north end to 30ft at the south end) was removed by steam digger (20-ton Ruston Proctor navvy) and all other operations were by hand. The overlying limestone was quarried for fluxing purposes and the iron ore was sold in a raw state to local furnaces. An Andrew Barclay Standard 14inch steam locomotive, inscribed 'JW Pain Whiston Mines' was supplied new in 1914. This was kept in a brick built loco shed at the top of the steepish (1:20) incline up from the Cogenhoe to Grendon Road. There is video footage of both this model of steam engine and steam digger on YouTube. The engine shed was afterwards used to store agricultural implements until falling into disrepair and was finally demolished in the 1970s.

In 1917, the quarry was acquired by Bloxham Ironstone Co Ltd on lease from their chairman Alfred Wassell. Eric Tonk's excellent book 'The Ironstone Quarries of the Midlands' states 'the agreement of 17th December 1917 records that Mr Wassell owner of the freehold property at Whiston has spent large sums in securing the connection to the LNWR, opening an extensive working face of stone, purchase of wagons, digger, conveyor, locomotive and plant.' This would appear to be claiming credit for JW Pain's efforts, but evidently Wassell was associated from the enterprise from the start, possibly as manager. The quarries were leased to Bloxham and Whiston for nineteen years from 29th September, 1917 with an option for a further seven years, at a royalty of 4d per ton.

The new operators were not very successful and in 1918 Pickering Phipps of Hunsbury Blast Furnaces Northampton acquired the Whiston Quarries. Hunsbury Ironworks were closed in 1920 and Whiston quarries ceased production in 1922. The locomotive was then stored at Hunsbury, where the photographs shown on the next few pages were taken in 1938. The sidings were removed in 1923. The quarry at Whiston was simply left in the derelict state, not even planted with trees.

Jim Pitts, the farmer who owned Moat Farm until his death in 2016, told me that the disruption caused by the noise and dust of quarrying, the rail line cutting the farm in two, and the succession of landlords, would have made Moat Farm almost untenable for the Blacklees in the early days of the 20th century.

Whiston Quarry's Andrew Barclay Standard 14in.
Locomotive, purchased new in 1914

No. 5 Transporter at Whiston Quarry, 1916

No. 20 Ruston Proctor navvy

Wellingborough Ironworks in 1905

Whiston quarry was left derelict after limestone extraction

11. Farmer to Surveyor
Phil Blacklee, born 1919

My father Phil's earliest memory (recalled recently at the age of ninety-eight!) was of standing up in his cot at Moat Farm and looking out of the window overlooking the village green. Also, he remembers whilst still a toddler, 'escaping' to investigate a commotion in the farm yard behind the house. His father Wilf had turned a pig on its back and was in the process of slitting its throat prior to butchering. Phil's mother Olive came tearing out of the house in a vain attempt to prevent him from witnessing the grizzly scene. Phil was to quickly learn that such activities were the way of life when growing up on a small farm.

Phil was educated at Derngate Junior School and Northampton Grammar School. United Counties or York's buses would collect the school children from outlying villages during term time, otherwise they cycled. Phil says his schooling in Northampton ensured he always had plenty of friends despite living out in the rural countryside. During his formative years Phil lived at Moat Farm, Whiston, Furze Farm, Brafield-on-the-Green and Maryland Farm, Grendon.

His parents' good friends, the Richardsons, (who were builders by trade) had talked him out of staying on the farm and recommended him to Ernest Howard's father, a Quantity Surveyor in Northampton for a job. Phil took it and rode his motorcycle into Northampton every day. He still remembers dropping off his mother's dressed cockerels to customers on the way to work. One day Phil had a lucky escape when a motorist leaving the Royal Oak public house in Cogenhoe crashed into his bike, ripping off the rear number plate.

Wilf Blacklee with baby Phil in 1920

Phil Blacklee in the army

Phil had created a study area in a corner of the stone barn at Maryland Farm Grendon for homework for his surveying exams. He shared the barn with pigs and poultry, the pigs on the farm being his responsibility at the time. Sometimes, he recollects fondly, a local lass would creep in quietly and attempt to distract him from his studies! This was shortly before the Second World War. During his wartime service Phil, together with another trainee surveyor from his regiment, were called into service when anything needed surveying. This included scouting out and mapping potential landing

strips, gun emplacements and sites suitable for building
military camps. This hands-on experience convinced
Phil that practical building surveying was much more
interesting than quantity surveying and he changed
disciplines before his finals.

LCM Shop in 1931

Head office in Market Square, Northampton 1964

Phil continued with his studies after the war and qualified as a Chartered Surveyor in 1947. He had married Sylvia in 1945 (chapter 15) and they were living at Number 11, Fullingdale Road, Northampton. Daughter Sheila had recently been born and Phil joined London Central Meat Company which was based in the town. LCM as they were generally known had been started in Tamworth in the 1890s by a Mr Lea and Mr Lowe. Arthur Baxter married Mr Lea's daughter and built up the business dealing in home killed and imported meat. When Phil Blacklee joined there were a significant number of butcher's shops in the group but no abattoirs or depots. The shops were mainly located in poor trading positions. Phil's job was to acquire prime shops and dispose of the secondary ones, also to arrange for the building of abattoirs and depots. In the early days, abattoirs were built at Hardingstone and Gloucester, and depots in Chester and Southampton. The portfolio of butcher's shops grew to around 400, although the total freehold estate was closer to 1000. Sometimes the company were offered more than one shop at a time and those they didn't need for butcher's shops were let. In 1964, the name was changed to Baxter's Butchers Ltd and new offices were constructed at the bottom of Albion Place in Northampton to replace the offices above a butcher's shop in Market Square. In 1974, Baxter's were acquired by Brooke Bond Oxo and in 1982 they became Unilever. In less than a year, Unilever only wanted the tea and coffee business and 260 shops and depots were sold to Union International (Vestey) trading as Dewhurst who went into receivership in 1995 after 100 years on the high street.

Phil was estates director of Baxter's Butchers for many years until retirement in 1982. He spent a lot of his work time travelling. It was nothing for him to drive to the furthest towns and back in a day. Sometimes when travelling near Taunton or Llandudno he would stay with one of his uncles, Dr Bert or Dr Fred. When my brother Andrew became a retail surveyor he was most impressed by Phil's encyclopaedic knowledge of shopping streets throughout the country, even long after retirement.

After two years of living at Fullingdale Road, Phil and Sylvia attended an auction at The Plough public house in East Haddon. They successfully bid for Rose Cottage opposite the church. That was in 1949 and Phil still lives there today. He often tells the story of a man who arrived too late for the auction and offered him an immediate profit for the house. His car had suffered a puncture on the way to the auction. Fortunately, Phil refused the offer as Rose Cottage has proved to be a very good buy for the family.

12. The Man Who Met Hitler
Harold Laurance, 1915-2004

My father Phil Blacklee remembers growing up at Brafield-on-the-Green with great affection. He was friendly with the local gamekeeper and spent many happy hours with him learning country ways. Phil and his mother Olive would cycle into Brafield and leave their bikes at Johnson's garage or Bailey's Co-op shop whilst they took the bus into Northampton, Bedford or Olney. Phil often cycled the six miles from Furze Farm to Northampton Grammar School with his friend Harold Laurance. They would sometimes race the school bus. Harold was a super fit bodybuilder who claimed to be the strongest man in England. His family farmed at Roundhay Farm, Yardley Hastings. Harold, four years older than Phil, is described as 'a Greek God' in the British Pathe production *The Statue Lives 1936* (which can be viewed on YouTube). This short documentary gives a good impression of Northamptonshire farm life in the 1930s, with pigs and poultry running free, Harold posing in a pony and trap, etc. I was told Harold Laurance represented England at the 1936 Berlin

Summer Olympics. I have checked this and found that Harold was indeed present and was the youngest British participant aged twenty-one. He came 12th in weightlifting and shook hands with Adolf Hitler! The story goes that Hitler took a shine to the blonde-haired, blue-eyed Laurance.

Harold was a notorious womaniser before the war but infamously scooted back to the family farm as soon as hostilities were declared to avoid being called up. Apparently, this was all the talk of Yardley Hastings at the time! Harold later had a frozen food business called Blue Riband. His freezers were kept in a barn at Avenue Farm, Yardley Hastings where the 'rent' comprised 'as much food as the occupants - the Winter family - could eat from Harold's freezers!'

Harold Laurance was born on 1st July 1915 in Yardley Hastings and died in Kettering in January 2004

13. The V1 Flying Bomb Incident

Phil Blacklee applied to join the RAF at the outbreak of the Second World War but was rejected from flying training on medical grounds. He apparently had one tonsil larger than the other! Instead, he was enlisted into the army as a heavy gunner with the Royal Artillery. His enlistment was deferred by a couple of months to enable him to complete a preliminary surveying exam. He used the time to make himself fit and to wear in his army boots by helping the Spencers of Grendon Manor Farm with the harvest. Phil was driving a horse and cart laden with hay one day when machine gunned by an enemy airman. The horse bolted and the cart crashed, but fortunately Phil was unhurt. This happened in the field opposite Sweetacre on Yardley Road. The incident was remembered years later when spent bullets were recovered from the field in the 1980s by archaeologist Roy Turland, who was metal detecting the site of a former Roman Villa. This wartime incident is recorded in more detail in an article on the Grendon parish website.

Phil rose to the rank of captain in the army. He was transferred from Aberdeen to the south coast to take charge of a gun battery tasked with trying to shoot down some of the 9,500 German V1 flying bombs targeted at London. Sometimes, these buzz bombs or doodlebugs as they were known would fly over too low to shoot at, hitting the cliffs or the ground or trees and exploding well short of their intended targets. Phil recalls one near miss in particular when a 400 mph V1 just cleared the white cliffs and was heading directly towards his gun battery when it hit a tree and blew up. Normally anti-aircraft batteries comprised four guns, but this was a six-gun battery in view of the great threat faced by this first line of defence location.

The code name for the campaign of operations against all phases of the German long-range weapons programme was 'Operation Crossbow.'

Phil Blacklee is fourth from left, with 3.7inch anti-aircraft gun.
The year is about 1940

A flying bomb

14. The Stirling Bomber Crash of 1941

By coincidence, the wartime crash of a heavy bomber in Northampton links Gold St, where the Blacklees had their outfitter's shop, with Billing Road cemetery where various members of the Blacklee and Longland families (chapter 26) are reputedly buried.

On the 14th/15th July, 1941 a 30-ton Stirling bomber, N6033, took part in Operation Hanover, flying out of Oakington aerodrome near Cambridge. The aircraft was damaged by flak over enemy territory and attempted to return home complete with some of the 8-ton bomb load. Flying over Northamptonshire, fuel ran low and the engines started to misfire, but no suitable landing site could be found. Bombs were jettisoned and fell onto Billing Road cemetery, perhaps the only open area of land in sight, in anticipation of a crash landing. The crew bailed out successfully, apart from the pilot who slipped from his parachute and fell to his death in Kingsthorpe Rec. He was found in the morning by a paper man on his rounds. The abandoned aircraft circled the town before crashing into Gold Street at 5.15am. Miraculously, very little damage ensued although the 100ft wingspan caused buildings on both sides of the street to be scraped on the plane's journey up the hill towards All Saints church (which in the 13th century had been almost as big as Westminster Abbey). Unexploded bombs and wreckage were strewn in the area of Gold Street/College Street, just where Blacklees shop was located adjacent to the Royal Hotel.

The wreckage strewn around the top of Gold Street and Bridge Street in front of the church. Unexploded bombs are clearly visible lying on the road.

Quite why the crew didn't jettison the bombs over the sea has not been reported. Perhaps the damage the plane sustained prevented normal bomb release. The chief constable of Northampton is said to have phoned the station commander at Oakington to complain, reputedly saying, 'I can't be having this in my town!'

I first learned of the cemetery incident whilst carrying out a survey of a 1930s semi-detached house on Barry Road in the 1980s. I was mystified by a pattern of cracks in the house which were not consistent with normal settlement. Further enquiries revealed it was bomb damage from the war years. I believe this was the only wartime bombing incident in Northampton. Oakington is now a high security reception centre used for screening immigrants.

Stirling bomber

15. The Gimson Connection

Shortly after arrival at his new army posting, an anti-aircraft battery on the south coast of England (chapter 13) Phil Blacklee encountered a pretty young ATS (Auxiliary Territorial Service) girl. She was visibly upset as she walked the 300 yards or so from the guns to the mess hut. As officer in charge, Phil felt it was his duty to enquire the reason for her distress. This is how he met his future wife Sylvia Gimson who had just received bad news from home about her father Albert Yeomans Gimson. His furniture business 'had gone wrong.' Albert was 'very clever with his hands but not a very good businessman.' Phil comforted Sylvia in her time of need, and the rest is history as they say.

Phil and Sylvia married shortly after the end of the war, on 7th June 1945, at Knighton Parish Church St Mary Magdalene in Leicester. Phil's great friend Edward William Bank (Ted) Skinner (d 2007) from Lodge Farm, Easton Maudit was Best Man.

Miss Sylvia M. Gimson, 52, Stoughton-road, Leicest
Subaltern in the A.T.S., and Capt. F. A. Blacklee.
Northants, who were married at St. Mary.

Phil and Sylvia Blacklee in 1945

Phil and Sylvia at East Haddon in 2016

Phil and Ted used to cycle together into Northampton (before they had motorbikes) to check out the nightspots. Ted's eldest son Phillip continues to farm at Lodge Farm today.

Sylvia May Gimson was born to parents Albert Yeomans Gimson and Eva Gertrude May (née Bohling) on 4th May 1921. The family address at the time was Number 11, Herne Hill Mansions, London. Sylvia was baptised at St Pauls, Herne Hill on Sunday, 26th June 1921. The family moved to Leicester where Sylvia attended Portland House private school until the age of thirteen, then Wyggeston Grammar School for Girls. After leaving school she entered art college and studied fashion design. Like her mother, Sylvia became an artist and designer. She continued to make and alter her own clothes and hats until very late in life. At the time of Phil and Sylvia's marriage in 1945, the Gimson's address was 52, Stoughton Road, Leicester. Sometime afterwards, Sylvia's parents Albert and Eva moved back to London.

Albert Gimson was a junior member of the illustrious Gimson family in Leicester. Albert was the eighth child of William Gimson and Martha Williams. Martha was the tenth child of Samuel and Sarah Williams. Following Sarah's death in 1855 at the age of 34, Samuel remarried to Mary, and had a further eleven children! Samuel Williams, an ironmonger, was himself the seventh child out of fifteen. He died in Sleaford in 1905, aged ninety-two.

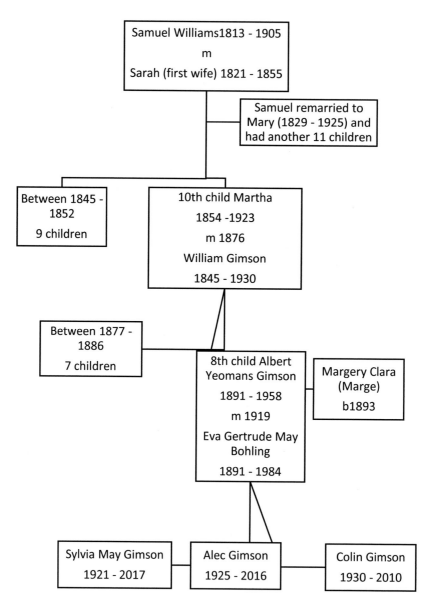

Samuel Williams 1813 - 1905

m

Sarah (first wife) 1821 - 1855

Samuel remarried to Mary (1829 - 1925) and had another 11 children

Between 1845 - 1852

9 children

10th child Martha

1854 -1923

m 1876

William Gimson

1845 - 1930

Between 1877 - 1886

7 children

8th child Albert Yeomans Gimson

1891 - 1958

m 1919

Eva Gertrude May Bohling

1891 - 1984

Margery Clara (Marge)

b1893

Sylvia May Gimson

1921 - 2017

Alec Gimson

1925 - 2016

Colin Gimson

1930 - 2010

Albert was descended from William's timber side of the family. As the second youngest of nine siblings, there was no opportunity for Albert within the business. After serving in the army at Gallipoli in the Great War (where he was shot in the shoulder), and a spell in Malaya afterwards growing pineapples, he established his own rather modest furniture making business. There was little love lost between Albert and his Leicester siblings and cousins in later life, as he felt they had basically 'thrown him out.'

Albert Gimson, having been wounded

The two branches of the Gimson family descended from Josiah and William ran very successful engineering and timber businesses in Leicester. Josiah established Vulcan Works for heavy engineering. There is an interesting video available on YouTube, 'the first public steaming of all four Gimson beam engines at Abbey pumping station, 2014' which gives an example of one of the company's achievements. Abbey pumping station is located close to the National Space Centre Corporation Rd Leicester LE4 5PX and is open to the public daily.

Eva Gimson modelling for husband Albert's catalogue

Albert, my grandfather, was a lovely man from what I can remember – tall, upright and very kind. Like many of the Gimsons, he was an excellent sportsman. As a child growing up at East Haddon, I had on my bedroom wall a number of caps awarded to him for, I think, rugby, cricket and rowing. I remember Albert and Eva living in a large dark house in Kew in the 1950s, at 108 Mortlake Road. He specialised at making furniture for needlework. Eva modelled for him and appeared on the cover of his catalogue. Later, my mother Sylvia became the model. Albert took the catalogue with him when he 'went round stores, shops, haberdashers and dear old lady craft shops' – my mother's words. At Christmas time, our grandparents came to Rose Cottage, East Haddon when we were children. Grandpa Gimson would take me down the village to Craddock bakers on Christmas morning to collect the enormous 25lb turkey (supplied by London Central Meat Co where my father worked) which had been cooked in the bread oven. After Albert's death in 1958, Eva lived in a first-floor maisonette at Number 4, St Mary's Close, Ewell. We would go and visit her occasionally and I always thought she must have been very lonely.

16. The Shipwreck
circa 1865

My grandmother Eva Gertrude May Gimson (née Böhling, b1891) was a young dress designer when she met Albert Gimson. I believe they married in London in 1919, although details of Eva's early years are sketchy. Eva had three elder sisters Adelaide, Maud and Marguerite, and two younger brothers Herman and Leslie. Maud married Bishop John Henry Blandford of the Moravian Church in 1915 and they had a daughter, Frances Blandford, who became a librarian. I cannot recollect being told anything much about this side of the family as a child and only learnt this information recently from my brother Andrew.

I have a faded copy of a marriage certificate dated 24th January, 1883 recording the marriage in the Moravian Church at 32 Fetter Street, London between Hermann Böhling, twenty-one, from Bow, commercial clerk, and Adelheid Franziska Kauffman, nineteen. The groom's father is shown as Gerd Böhling (deceased), a sugar refiner and the bride's father - (unknown first name) Kauffman (supposed deceased), a boot maker. The couple met through being fellow members of the Moravian Church at Fetter Lane. Hermann was much sought after as a pianist and organist. Music was an important part of the Moravian church. His father Gerd (born 1820) had come to England in about 1837. As the fourth son of a farmer, (Johan Hinrich Böhling, born 1781) Gerd had no prospect of inheriting the family farm located in a village 'near Bremen.' Many Böhlings still live in this area. The family had long ago fled Moravia (in what is now the Czech Republic) where Moravians were persecuted by the Catholics. They settled initially at Herrnhut, Upper Lusatia, where Germany, Poland and the Czech Republic meet. Herrnhut was founded in 1722 by Protestant religious refugees from Moravia on the estate of Count Nikolaus Ludwin von Zinzendorf. My brother Andrew and his wife Jill have recently visited Herrnhut and found it to be 'an austere, rather bleak town.'

The Moravian church in Fetter Lane London was destroyed in the Blitz during the Second World War.

The reason why the young bride Adelheid Kauffman (my great grandmother on my mother's side) didn't know much about her father can possibly be explained by notes left by Frances Blandford. Apparently the Kauffmans were emigrating to America around 1864 or 5, when Adelheid was still a baby, and their ship ran aground near Freshwater Bay on the Isle of Wight. Unfortunately, there is no record of the ship's port of departure, whether from Great Britain or Germany.

I have looked for records of shipwrecks around this time in this vicinity, but reliable information is very scarce. The National Life Boat Institution (forerunner of the RNLI) placed two lifeboats on the south west coast of the IOW in 1860 following three vessels and several lives being lost during the previous winter. Lying near the track of all vessels passing up or down the Channel, the coast on this part of the island has always been liable to wrecks.

There was apparently 'great loss of life including Adelheid's father.' A family called Mallalieu adopted Adelheid in London (presumably through Moravian Church connections), and later the Eiseler family took her in. The Eiseler's were 'something in Bond Street.' They were also connected with Flowers the brewers at Stratford East London. The girl's mother took her other daughters 'Peggy and Sue' back to Germany where

'Peggy' (I think it was) became an opera singer, a prima donna in St Petersburg (Leningrad) who visited Covent Garden with her opera. There was a Russian family connection further back, long before the revolution and Frances Blandford inherited a family crucifix of Russian origin. Francis had researched the Opera story and drawn a blank. She concluded the singer perhaps didn't use the name Kauffman. Also, the names Peggy and Sue were most likely anglicized versions of their given German names. The 1901 census shows the household of Hermann Bohling at Hainault Road, Low Leighton contained:

Hermann Bohling, age thirty-nine, born in Whitechapel.

Josephene LF Bohling, age thirty-six, born in Germany.

Maud, age fifteen, Marguerite, age eleven, Eva, age nine, Hermann, age eight, all born in Tottenham, and Leslie born in Leytonstone.

Presumably, Josephene is an anglicized version of Adelheid.

This is a work in progress, as I should like to find out more about the Kauffman family.

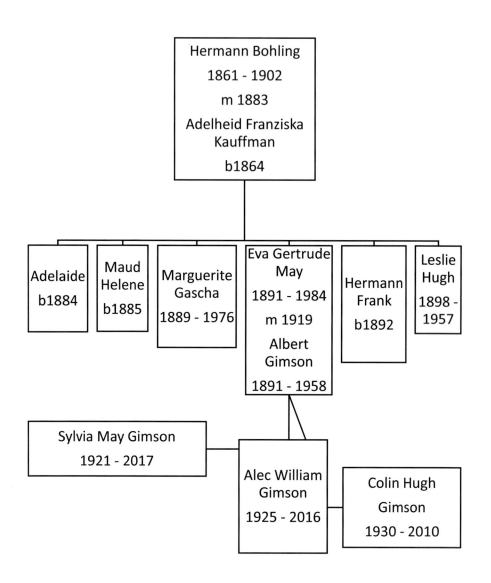

Hermann Bohling
1861 - 1902
m 1883
Adelheid Franziska Kauffman
b1864

Adelaide
b1884

Maud Helene
b1885

Marguerite Gascha
1889 - 1976

Eva Gertrude May
1891 - 1984
m 1919
Albert Gimson
1891 - 1958

Hermann Frank
b1892

Leslie Hugh
1898 - 1957

Sylvia May Gimson
1921 - 2017

Alec William Gimson
1925 - 2016

Colin Hugh Gimson
1930 - 2010

17. Second Military Cross
Captain Walter Stanley Gimson, 1885-1916

One of my grandfather Albert Gimson's older brothers Walter Stanley Gimson (born 1885) was a cabinet maker living and working in Nottingham at the outbreak of the Great War. His address was The Hawthorns, Dagmar Grove, Nottingham. He enlisted together with colleagues referred to as 'The Nottingham Athletes' into the tenth Battalion of the Notts and Derby Regiment, also known as the Sherwood Foresters. Walter was soon promoted to Sergeant and was hospitalised with a shrapnel wound in his side in France in December, 1915. Sergeant Gimson received his commission on 15th March, 1916 and was promoted to second lieutenant.

On the 2nd June, 1916 the German army launched an attack against the high ground of Mount Sorrel, close to Hooge to the east of the Ypres Salient. This was to draw British resources away from the Somme. Walter was transferred to the Yorkshire Light Infantry to command a front-line trench mortar battery. Trench mortars were known by the British as 'flying pigs' and were always certain to draw enemy fire. Walter was again promoted, to Captain, and awarded the Military Cross in 1917 after two years of continuous active service.

Capt. W. S. Gimson.
Awarded Military Cross.

Captain W S Gimson

He was killed at Langemarck on August 16th, 1917 during the Third Battle of Ypres, often referred to as Passchendaele. He was amongst 15,000 casualties for an advance of no more than 1,500 yards. He had been married for just seven weeks. Communicating the news of his death to his wife Isobel Beatrice (née Moss) a fellow officer wrote: 'Captain Gimson was one of the most popular officers in the division, and when killed in the advance towards Langemarck was acting like a hero.'

Captain Walter Stanley Gimson is buried at Bard Cottage Cemetery Boezinge. His grave reference: 1V B 48.

British Trench Mortar Team

18. The Famous Architect
Ernest Gimson, 1864–1919

DESIGNER: Ernest Gimson

One of my grandfather Albert Gimson's better remembered relations was Ernest Gimson, a protégé of William Morris of the Arts and Crafts movement.

Ernest Gimson was the second son of Josiah Gimson and his second wife Sarah. Ernest was described as 'a thinker, an explorer and a teacher whose chief aim was to bring some pride and joy into the work of the British working man.'

He became an architect, designer and craftsman who is remembered for a number of outstanding buildings and works of art in a wide range of materials. He had a hand in the buildings described in the following chapters.

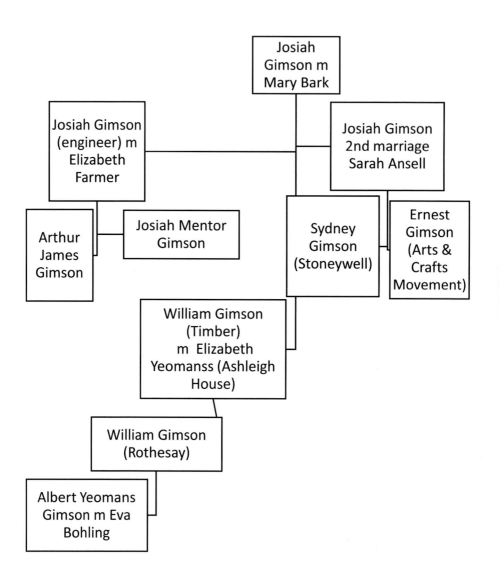

19. Ashleigh House
William Gimson, 1814–1901

Albert Gimson at Ashleigh House

William Gimson (1814–1901), founder of the Gimson timber company in 1834, and his wife Elizabeth (née Yeomans, 1814–1894) had Ashleigh House built for their family in 1871. And what a family it was, with thirteen children and fifty-five grandchildren! The Ashleigh House estate, located in what is now part of Christ the King School, Danehills, Leicester, comprised sixty-four acres.

Ashleigh was a very grand house crowned with wrought iron and had large reception rooms filled with antique furniture. Two of William and Elizabeth's granddaughters later wrote some recollections of their visits to the house when their grandparents were still alive:

'We were met at the main door by a maid and shown to the drawing room where my grandparents were resting in large high-backed upholstered chairs, a large log fire burning in the grate. There were lots of paintings on the walls and many ornaments. There was no electricity in the house and lighting was provided by gas mantles and oil lamps both with crinkled glass shades. When it got dark the maid came to light the gas and lamps with long coloured tapers. Tea was served on mahogany trays promptly at 4 o'clock by the maid but Granny Gimson always poured it into fine porcelain cups and saucers. Sugar was always cubed, not loose, except when used on fresh fruit sweets like strawberries.

I did not speak until spoken to and had to be on my best behaviour for the duration of the visit. The adults discussed business and current affairs, and occasionally aunts and uncles and their families.

I was sometimes allowed to go to the old nursery where Uncle Albert and mother's toys remained and I remember an old rocking horse, some jigsaw puzzles, a musical box and some building blocks which formed a picture when built correctly.

The hallway had a very large grandfather clock with a very loud tick which echoed eerily. It struck a ding-dong for each quarter and was followed by a louder bell on each hour.

The dining room had a very large table and twelve chairs with horsehair seats which always made our legs itch terribly. The whole house smelt of polish.

Ashleigh House had a beautiful walled garden for fruit and vegetables with lovely little box hedges around the beds. The red headed gardener was not a very nice person. He did not like children, especially little girls who wore blouses with elastic all round which made excellent hiding places for fruit.

William Gimson travelled everywhere by horse and carriage as there were no motor vehicles in those days. He wore a black silk top hat and a tail coat to work. The coachman was called Cleaver and he was very old and wrinkled. The carriage was entered by means of a step at the back.'

20. Rothesay
William Gimson Jnr, 1845-1930

Rothesay, located at University Road Leicester (formerly known as Victoria Road) was a fine house designed by the architect Joseph Goddard in the late 19th century. It was purchased by William Gimson (1814–1901, the founder of Gimson timber company) for his son and family shortly after it was built. The family consisting of William Gimson Jnr (1845–1930) and Martha (née Williams, 1854-1923), their nine children and servants remained there until 1930 when William Gimson Jnr died.

William Jnr's cousin was Ernest Gimson of the Arts and Crafts Movement, a student of William Morriss. Ernest designed the wall tiles for the bathrooms and fireplaces at Rothesay. The Four Seasons group of tiles in the main hall are said to have been specially commissioned by William Jnr to resemble his four daughters.

William Gimson with Sylvia at Rothesay Leicester in 1922

William Gimson Jnr was my mother's grandfather. When Sylvia Blacklee attended her grandfather's funeral in 1930 she was nine years old. Remembering the event in later life, she returned to search for the house in 1988 at the request of her younger brother Colin in Australia who was researching Gimson family history. Sylvia recollects her grandfather 'lay in state' in the drawing room for family members to pay their last respects. Fortunately, the coffin was too high up for her to see inside. The family were all in deepest black of course and the blinds drawn.

When Sylvia revisited in 1988, Numbers 8 to 12 University Road, Leicester were occupied by the City Division, Womans & Childrens Services. In true Sylvia style, she brazenly appeared at the reception desk one day to ask if the house next door was called 'Rothesay.' Neil Hatfield was called down to see her as his father was Company Secretary for William Gimson & Sons Ltd and had been employed by the firm since before the war. Neil was pleased to show Sylvia around the house where her father Albert Yeomans Gimson had been brought up as the youngest of five boys.

Sylvia could not recall ever staying with her grandfather at Rothesay, but remembered going into the attic rooms with a maid and seeing all her father's generation toys including a large rocking horse. She was delighted to be able to look around the rooms she had once played in as a child herself and was able to tell Neil of the times she would sit on the balustrade landing looking through at the giant Christmas tree with all its bare flamed candles in the hall below, and remembering family gatherings in a 'room with sunflowers somewhere near the ceiling' - the sort of detail a small child would remember. The sunflowers are painted on the top of the over mantle in the garden room, and to Sylvia's delight, were still there in 1988, in the room used by the senior medical officers.

21. Stoneywell - a National Trust property

Author's wife, Carolyn and son, Edward Blacklee at
Stoneywell in 2016

A Gimson weekend retreat north of Leicester,
Stoneywell in Charnwood Forest, was built by the
architect Ernest Gimson for his elder brother Sydney in
1899. It is now owned by the National Trust and was

opened to the public in February 2015. The National Trust's description captures the scene: 'Set in an enchanted part of Leicestershire Stoneywell is the perfect adventure house with its light filled rooms, warren of twisting stairs and surprising angles.' Stoneywell is certainly well worth a visit and needs to be booked in advance.

22. The 7-foot bed
Christopher Gimson, 1886-1975

Christopher Gimson C.I.E, I.C.S. was born in Leicester on 24th December, 1886. He was an outstanding English cricketer active from 1908–1921 who played for Cambridge University and Leicestershire. He appeared in nine first class matches as a right-handed batsman who scored 175 runs with a highest score of forty. He also played tennis for Leicestershire.

He played rugby football for Leicester Tigers and the Barbarians and had the distinction of playing in the first rugby match ever to be played at Twickenham, and the first Leicestershire/Barbarian rugby football match ever to be played at Leicester. Christopher was exceptionally tall and his uncle Ernest Gimson made a special 7-foot single oak bed for him, which was donated to Leicester Museum in 1988.

He was a member of the famous Leicester family who made their fortune in the Vulcan Iron Foundry and engineering works but also spearheaded the Arts and

Crafts movement and also were founders of Leicester Secular Society the oldest Secular Society in the world.

Christopher was educated at Stonygate School in Leicester before attending Oundle in 1900 and Emmanuel College Cambridge, where he obtained his Batchelor of Arts Degree in Classics. He worked in the Indian Civil Service, much of his time being spent in Manipur State as Political Agent. He was made Companion of the Order of the Indian Empire in 1943 and died in Leicester on the 8th of November, 1975.

23. Third Military Cross
Major Richard Gimson, 1922-2018

INTO BATTLE: Left, Allied troops land at Salerno in 1943, where Major Richard Gimson, above, a platoon commander with 571 Army Field Company Royal Engineers, was honoured for gallantry

Major Richard Gimson

Major Richard Allynne Stanford Gimson who died aged ninety-five in January 2018 was the great grandson of Josiah Gimson, who established the family engineering business in Vulcan Works in Leicester in the mid-19th century. Educated at Uppingham and Clare College Cambridge, he won the Military Cross in 1943 in the Italian campaign. Gimson was a platoon commander with 571 Army Field Company Royal Engineers (RE). Of the seven officers who landed at Salerno in September 1943 with the first batch of sappers, six became casualties. His tank landing craft had been strafed by German fighters and it took three attempts to get ashore. Their job was to clear mines and ensure the port was made available for shipping whilst he and his men were under constant shelling, mortar fire and sniping and took heavy casualties. They successfully completed the task within a couple of weeks.

Later his platoon came under relentless mortar fire whilst constructing a bridge across the river Volturno at Grazzanise. Major Gimson was awarded the MC for exemplary gallantry during active operations against the enemy and his inspiring leadership throughout the campaign.

During the Second Battle of Alamein he had to crawl through an allied minefield to lift and defuse enemy mines whilst enveloped in clouds of sand and metal and with the ground shaking from a huge artillery barrage. Gimson was captured by the Italians but managed to escape by wearing an Italian uniform he liberated and using schoolboy Latin when challenged.

After the war he worked for a number of engineering companies including Ruston & Hornsby, who made mechanical shovels and diggers for quarrying. In 1977 he started a company on the Suffolk coast to explore alternative energy sources, long before it became fashionable.

In 1987, Richard and his wife Elspeth (née Ogilvie) set up the Warden's Trust to provide recreational facilities for disabled children and adults. He was made a MBE in 2007 for services to the disabled. Richard Gimson was my third cousin once removed.

24. Black Christmas
Sir Franklin Gimson, 1890-1976

Sir Franklin Gimson

Governor of Singapore

Another notable family member is my mother Sylvia Blacklee's ninth cousin Sir Franklin Charles Gimson. He was born on 19th September 1890 in Barrow-on- Soar, Leicestershire, to the Rev. Charles Keightley Gimson. Gimson graduated Balliol College Oxford with a

Bachelor of Arts degree and entered the British Ceylon Civil Service in 1914. He was attached to the office of Naval Intelligence during the Great War (1914–1918).

In 1941, during the Second World War, he was promoted to the post of Colonial Secretary of Hong Kong. Extremely unfortunate timing saw Gimson arrive at the colony on 7th December, the day before the Japanese Army invaded. The undermanned defence forces soon lost the Battle of Hong Kong and the Governor surrendered the Colony on 25th December 1941, a date thereafter known as 'Black Christmas.' British officials and civilians alike were arrested and sent to Stanley Internment Camp at St Stephen's College on the southern end of Hong Kong Island. Camp conditions were appalling with no prepared facilities and inmates were left to care largely for themselves. Any food supplied by the captors was 'of poor quality, frequently containing dust, mud, rat and cockroach excreta, cigarette ends and sometimes dead rats.'

As Colonial Secretary, Gimson was responsible for negotiating with the Japanese on matters relating to the camp. This must have been a dreadful job with 121 internees dying in the camp before the Emperor of Japan finally announced an unconditional surrender to the Allies on 15th August, 1945. Many interns died of illness, seven were publicly executed by the Japanese by shooting or beheading, and the Americans bombed hut 5 by mistake on 16th January 1945, killing fourteen. After the Japanese surrender, the Americans offered Hong

Kong to China. Fortunately, Gimson was on hand to exercise the sovereignty on behalf of the British government. Gimson, although severely emaciated after years of internment, declared himself 'Acting Governor' and was sworn in by the Chief Justice. Shortly afterwards the British Fleet arrived and Gimson transferred power to Rear Admiral Cecil Harcourt. The military government was officially formed on 1st September, retaining the status of the British Hong Kong Colony.

Gimson was appointed Governor of Singapore between 1946 and 1952 after which he retired. My brother Andrew has recently visited the city state of Singapore where the name of Gimson remains legendary, appearing on faded shop fronts and even on packaged food products!

25. Post-war Life at Maryland Farm

Returning to the Blacklees (from chapter 7), my grandparents, Wilf and Olive Blacklee were always very active in the community and well-liked by those who met them. Helen O'Neill (chapter 40) kept several of their letters from friends and neighbours thanking them for their kindness and assistance.

Dr James Warren Dodson (born 1938) of Bath remembers Maryland Farm Grendon in the 1950s. His mother Winifred (Win) was Bernard Smith's sister. Bernard married my auntie Molly.

I am very grateful to Dr James Dodson for providing the following reminiscences of post war life on the farm:

'I knew them (Olive and Wilf) as the parents of my Uncle Bernard's wife, Molly Smith, (née Blacklee). I was taught to call them Mr & Mrs Blacklee. I knew she (Molly) had a brother Phil but I only met him a few times. My mother Winifred Martha Dodson (née Smith) was the younger sister of Bernard Henry Smith who married Molly Blacklee. My father had died when I was a baby and, looking back, I think Uncle Bernard was a great support for my mother. We often went over on the bus to Home Farm Little Oakley. I was fifteen or sixteen when Bernard and Molly moved to Grendon. By then I was working in the school holidays at the family firm in Ringstead, S.W. Dodson Ltd, later Dodson & Horrell, horse feed specialists. I have faint memories of Wilf, he was tall and thin and had a grey moustache, a kind man, but I think he died soon after Bernard and Molly moved there. My most striking memory associated with him is that he had a Riley car, circa 1937, which was kept in a barn. I recollect Mr Blacklee was no longer driving it. It had dark blue upholstery, perhaps the body was dark blue. I was very impressed with it (I had a Riley myself later on, but mine was 1952, not as exotic and exciting as Mr Blacklee's). Bernard and Molly had the southern end of the house, including the kitchen, and Mrs Blacklee (as I knew her) had the northern part including the main sitting room. There was a flat roofed extension on the eastern side that was the living room for Bernard and Molly. I think perhaps that it was built especially for them. It had a small fireplace and I thought it was rather a cold room (it was 1950s Britain and probably money was very tight). The main part of the house was thatched and I remember moss on it and holes made by sparrows and it was re-thatched shortly after Bernard & Molly moved in. I have been calling my aunt Molly in this letter. I think that may have been what Mrs Blacklee called her, but in my family, we always referred to her as Aunty Moll. I am trying to recall what Uncle Bernard called her. I think he usually said 'Moll' but occasionally 'Molly.' When we visited Grendon to see Uncle Bernard and Auntie Moll, we would always go through to see Mrs Blacklee, and she would usually give us a slice of home-made cake. My memories of her are of her being kind and affectionate. I recall being struck by her saying, when asked what she was doing these days, that she took Meals on Wheels to 'the old people.' As she was well over sixty at the time that struck me as funny, because clearly, she was old (I was probably about ten) and apparently, she did not realise it! Now, at seventy-nine, I have a different view. I remember Uncle Bernard pointing out to me a well in the garden about four to six paces east of the house at Maryland Farm. It was capped over with concrete, so that no-one could fall down it, but before piped water came to Grendon, that must have been the main source of drinking water for the house. Bernard said it had never failed to have some water in it, but in dry years the level went low and he had been down it: my memory is that he said the chamber was big enough to turn around a horse and cart but writing that now I wonder if my boyish memory exaggerated a bit and perhaps he said 'big enough for a horse and cart.' Even so that is a pretty big volume.'

Dr James Dodson's recollections of life at Maryland Farm nicely sum up my own memories. I don't remember the Riley car but I clearly recollect my grandmother Olive telling me the horse and cart story about the well. She told me you could turn around a horse and cart at the bottom so it must have been an enormous 'bell' well. When Helen's builder husband Kieran O'Neill (chapter 39) and his colleague Albert Lester from Mears Ashby demolished the unstable two-storey northern extension of Maryland Farm House in the 1980s, (which had been built for Wilf & Olive in the 1930s) the whole lot went down that well and it was still not filled up all the way to the top.

Ann Benady (neé Bowers) (chapter 37) of Grendon remembers spending nearly every Sunday with her 'Auntie Ol' Blacklee whilst her five brothers were away in the services. They welcomed each other's companionship. Ann would go into the end bedroom and watch Auntie plait her long hair. Together they did the church flowers, and regularly replaced the flowers on Olive's brother Douglas' war memorial. Ann helped with collecting the eggs from the chickens and ducks, and with other daily tasks around the farm.

Olive looked after the poultry, which was a very important contribution to the finances on the farm. Eggs were stored in the pantry. The door from the yard to the farm kitchen was always unlocked (there was no lock!), indeed, it was usually left wide open. Customers would walk down two steps into the kitchen, and up two steps on the left and into the pantry. This was always cool, with bare stone walls and stone thralls (shelves) for storing produce. A sheep dog or two and numerous cats

(I can remember up to nine at any one time) would be vying for the attention of visitors in the hope of a treat.

Neighbouring farmers including the Hopes (Villa Farm) and the Allebones of Easton Maudit were frequent visitors, almost part of the family. 'Uncle' Dick Allebone was Olive's god father.

Maryland Farm had frontage to Easton Way. Wilf and Olive were able to sell off a few building plots for housing over the years, including what is now the Sharplands estate. This enabled them to keep the farm going during very difficult times. Eventually Phil, fearing there would be no inheritance left, arranged a £1750 loan from Lloyds Bank for his parents to save them having to dispose of any more of the farm.

Olive was a well-practised cook. I remember her drop scones in particular as outstanding. The evening meal would be put in her little electric oven before she retired to bed for a rest in the afternoons. She had suffered a 'turn' when about eighteen and the doctor had recommended she take a rest after lunch. The family assumed the doctor had meant for a day or two but Olive heeded his advice for the rest of her life. By the time she emerged at teatime the pork chops, or whatever she was preparing, would be absolutely perfect. I used to stay at Grendon regularly as a child as my parents were often away and I loved my Gran's cooking. Only the finest china and cleanest table cloths and napkins would be on the table. Another treat I remember was fresh cow's milk still steaming from the milking parlour. I doubt that would be regarded as very safe today.

Wilf and Olive couldn't usually go on holiday together; someone had to remain on the farm to care for the animals and hens. After Bernard and Molly came to live at Maryland farm in 1954 or 5, Olive had more time to go on outings with York's coaches from Cogenhoe, with the other ladies of Grendon WI.

Olive outlived her husband, her daughter and son in law and remained living alone at Maryland Farm House until the age of ninety. She was aided by her neighbours Rachel (1916–2004) and Jack (1918-2007) Underwood who lived in the bungalow opposite.

Olive Blacklee spent the final ten years of her life in Oakwood nursing home in Northampton. She died on 11th January 1990, 6 months short of her 100th birthday. Her ashes were interred in Grendon churchyard on the 19th January and her headstone rests on Jane Longland's grave. The little headstone also records the passing of her husband Wilf in 1958 and daughter Molly in 1976.

26. The Longland Connection

James Herbert (JH) Longland with his sisters,
Annie and Polly

Their father, James Longland

Young Wilf Blacklee (my grandfather) went to live with the Longlands at Grendon Manor farm after his father's death in 1891. James Herbert (JH) Longland was the tenant farmer at the time. The farm comprised part of Lord Northampton's Castle Ashby estate. JH's father, another James, had died in 1875 when JH was about fifteen. His father's executors took over the tenancy of Manor farm until JH came of age. JH Longland continued the tenancy until his death in 1920 at the age of fifty-nine. JH was educated at Olney and Ullesthorpe schools and was buried next to his mother Jane Longland (née Wiggins), who died at the age of eighty-one in 1913. Wilf would have been twenty-six when his grandmother Jane died, the year before he married my grandmother Olive Bowers.

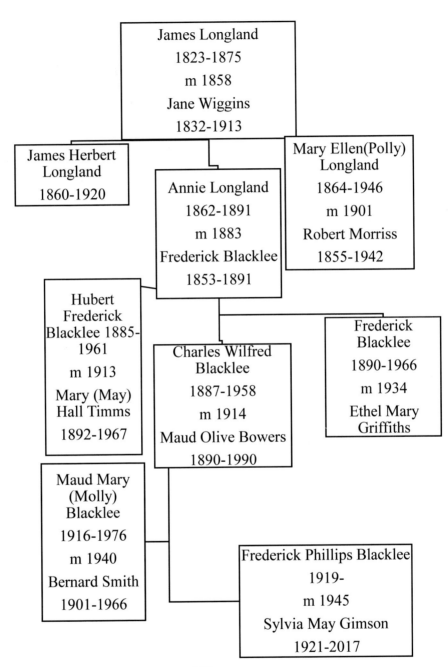

James Longland
1823-1875
m 1858
Jane Wiggins
1832-1913

James Herbert
Longland
1860-1920

Annie Longland
1862-1891
m 1883
Frederick Blacklee
1853-1891

Mary Ellen(Polly)
Longland
1864-1946
m 1901
Robert Morriss
1855-1942

Hubert
Frederick
Blacklee 1885-
1961
m 1913
Mary (May)
Hall Timms
1892-1967

Charles Wilfred
Blacklee
1887-1958
m 1914
Maud Olive Bowers
1890-1990

Frederick
Blacklee
1890-1966
m 1934
Ethel Mary
Griffiths

Maud Mary
(Molly)
Blacklee
1916-1976
m 1940
Bernard Smith
1901-1966

Frederick Phillips Blacklee
1919-
m 1945
Sylvia May Gimson
1921-2017

Grendon Manor Farmhouse in the 1930s

By all accounts, the Longlands were very successful farmers. An undated newspaper article, from before the Great War, gives an illuminating insight into life on the farm.

JH Longland is described as being 'of a singularly quiet, modest and unassuming nature.' His mother 'a very lovable lady, who despite her advancing years, maintains a deep interest in the affairs with which her son is concerned.' JH devoted a lot of his time to the discharge of public duties in local and district government.

Although Manor House Farm was the Marquess of Northampton's only property in Grendon his Lordship invited village people to attend any festivities taking place at Castle Ashby. Grendon residents were permitted to show exhibits at the prestigious annual Castle Ashby flower show, enjoying notable success. The farm reached out to the south west and south of Grendon and included fields on both sides of Yardley Hastings road. The 24-acre-28 perch field below the Manor House was known as Hungry Hill or Hanging Hill. It would be interesting to know the origins of these names. Locals would have been well aware of all the field names at the time. Meadows bordering the River Nene were highly prized for the hay crop, the rest of the land before the Enclosure Acts of earlier centuries would have been mostly big fields divided into furlongs. These furlongs were further divided into parallel acre or half acre strips, a one-acre strip being four rods (22 yards) in length. Unploughed paths or balks were left for common access and the parallel strips ended in headlands running the length of the fields. Field tenants in those days shared the good land with the bad, thus sometimes holding several strips in various fields.

The Manor House is described in the article as being 'a delightful old English residence of considerable dimensions.' It enjoys 'glorious views of Castle Ashby its park and lakes in one direction, long sweeps of the Nene valley in the other.' The farm is described as being 'very tidy and splendidly equipped.' The 250 acres being divided about equally between arable and pasture, the latter being good grazing. As the land is heavy, the Longlands kept a large number of horses.

James Longland Snr had enjoyed considerable success exhibiting livestock at county shows. His Shorthorn cattle and Oxford Down sheep won many prizes. Paintings of some of the animals adorned the walls of the Manor House. Phil Blacklee has an 1871 oil painting of one of the prize-winning Oxford Down rams at East Haddon. JH Longland didn't exhibit livestock himself but took a keen interest in attending agricultural shows as an official. In 1905 JH Longland was awarded a silver cup by a Wellingborough firm of maltsters 'for the best dressed barley.' I have this impressive cup in my modest 'museum' of family artefacts in Grendon.

Wilf is also mentioned in the newspaper article. 'Mr Longland is fortunate in having as his assistant his nephew Mr Wilfred Blacklee, the son of a late revered Northampton tradesman, who is learning the business and who takes an intelligent and active part in the management.'

JH Longland was a sound Liberal, a mainstay of the local Progressives. 'He and his mother kept non-conformity alive against stiff odds.' On Sundays they attended Yardley Hastings Congregational Church in the morning and Grendon Union Chapel in the afternoon.

JH Longland died in March 1920. The first part of his funeral service took place at the Union Chapel, Grendon, conducted by Rev A Martindale of Yardley Hastings. The service at the graveside in St Mary's Churchyard,

Grendon was conducted by the vicar, Rev AP Wodehouse. There had been a similar arrangement in March 1913 when James' mother Jane died. The first part of the funeral service was held at the Union Chapel (conducted by Rev E Palmer of Yardley Hastings). The cortege was met at the church gates by the vicar, the (very same) Rev AP Wodehouse. The coffin was borne by six of the farm employees.

The executors wasted no time in selling off James' livestock. Amongst family archives are Peirce & Thorpe's priced auction catalogue from 20th April 1920. Sixty-six 'exceedingly well bred' Shorthorn cattle, sixty-one Oxford Down sheep, four horses and fourteen pigs sold for £1875. Ninety-six acres of grass keeping fetched £386. There was a second auction on 28th September, 1920 for the household furniture, agricultural implements and machines, fifteen head of wintering cattle, eleven working horses, four unbroken fillies, three cart foals and sixty-five head of poultry.

The death of JH Longland was the end of the Longland's century-plus long tenure of Grendon Manor House Farm. It also sadly ended the Longland's involvement with our family. JH Longland had never married. Both his parents and sister Annie were dead, and his other sister, Mary Ellen (Polly) Morriss, died childless in 1946, aged eighty-two.

Manor House Farm was taken over by the Burns and then the Spencers. When Mr Burns retired from farming he built a bungalow opposite Maryland Farm. His wife didn't like him smoking his pipe at home, so he used to frequently pop over the road to see the Blacklees. Olive let him smoke in her house. Phil Blacklee remembers Mr Burns as 'a very nice man.'

The Spencers who took over Manor House Farm were two brothers, one was called Eric. They were thought to be unrelated to the Spencers of Hall Farm who were involved in the Battle of Grendon in 1876 (chapter 30). One of the brothers went to The Home Farm, East Haddon, where the family continue to farm.

Manor House is often referred to as 'Spencer's Farm' even today, although the Spencers are long departed from Grendon.

The Longland family was very prolific and successful and no doubt live on somewhere to this day through other branches. In 1980 Gran (Olive Blacklee) received correspondence from a John Longland of Hargrave, Chester. As Gran was ninety at the time, my father Phil replied on her behalf. John thought he may be descended from the first James Longland of Manor House, who had a son named John.

JH and his mother, Jane Longland, have magnificent headstones located to the immediate west of the Norman entrance porch at St Mary's Church, Grendon. The ashes of Wilf and Olive Blacklee and their daughter Molly Smith are buried with them. The two adjoining headstones are for Mary, widow of a previous James

Longland who died in 1901 (three or four James' had farmed over the years at Grendon Manor House Farm), and Thomas Longland, who may have been buried in 1874 (the inscription is eroded and all but illegible). It wasn't until my recent research that I realised my great grandmother Maud Mary Bowers (née Phillips 1860–1898), and my great-great grandmother Jane Longland (née Wiggins 1832–1913), are buried in adjacent plots in Grendon churchyard.

Church Lane, Grendon in 2018.

There are a further dozen Longland headstones in Yardley Hastings churchyard. My father Phil remembers a family of Longlands who ran a public House, the Northampton Arms, later the Shoulder of

Mutton, in Yardley. This is now Peter Grigg's house 'Longacre', where body builder Harold Laurance (chapter 12) lived for a while. At one time, the Longlands ran all three pubs in Yardley Hastings. Now there are two: the Red Lion (Charles Wells) and the Rose and Crown (Freehouse).

Bowers (on left) and four Longland/Blacklee headstones in St Mary's churchyard, Grendon.

27. The BBC Star
Sir Jack Longland 1905-1993

Longland: all-round champion

John Longland (chapter 26) told my father in the 1980 correspondence that his own father was Sir Jack Longland and his grandfather Ernest Henry Longland, a Church of England vicar, mostly in Worcestershire. Sir Jack was a Cambridge blue (pole vaulting), accomplished

121

mountaineer, educationalist and broadcaster. My grandmother Olive Blacklee remembered him coming to Grendon before the war to visit his relatives. His obituary in the Telegraph described him as 'a man who could stomach neither fools nor pomposity and was quite capable of savaging either when they crossed his path.' There was another side to his character which was more frequently to the fore - 'a delightful impishness, a relish for the robust ambiguity and the subtle pun.' This made Sir Jack an ideal choice as chairman and long-running question-master of the radio programme *My Word.* He presided over the BBC show from 1956 to 1976. Sir Jack's mother, Emily Rose, was the daughter of Sir James Crockett of Dallington Lodge, Northampton. Crockett is a well-known name in the shoe trade in Northampton. Sir James was a great supporter of Northampton General Hospital. Crockett and Jones is still a prestigious shoe maker in the town, with a number of retail shops.

28. The International Rugby Player
Ray Longland, 1908-1975

Phil Blacklee believes RJ (Ray) Longland, the RAF, Northampton and England rugby prop forward, is related to the family through the farming Longlands. Ray was born at nearby Lavendon in 1908. He was captain of the RAF rugby team during the war. He made

356 appearances for Northampton Saints (as captain in 1936 and 1947) and played nineteen international games for England. John Merry of Grendon remembers Ray Longland very well. John played for the Northampton RFC third team, the Crusaders ('The Crews'), and occasionally the seconds, The Wanderers ('The Wandies'). As Ray Longland was reaching the end of his playing career he enjoyed 'social' games with the Wandies and the Crews. John says that Ray always particularly enjoyed the post-match get together in the bar. John Merry's grandfather was the Merry who founded the well know auctioneering business in Northampton, where I worked in the 1980s.

29. The Bowers family - before the Great War

The family tree for the Bower's family commences with John Bowers (Yeoman of Willoughby Warcs) who married Elizabeth Lord of Barby, Northants in 1720. 'Yeoman' in this context probably means a commoner who cultivates his own land, a small landowner, a farmer of the middle classes. They had four children, Henry (Yeoman), Mary who married a William Grudgen, John Bowers, and Ruth 'who married a man with the surname Spencer.'

The third child, John Bowers, had a son who was also called John and lived in Braunston, Northamptonshire and married Ann Fleckenhoe. John and Ann had five children between the years 1780-1790. The youngest, Richard Bowers of Braunston (1790–1856), miller and baker, is my direct ancestor.

Braunston is located three miles north west of Daventry and stands close to Welton station on the former main line of the London and North Western Railway. The village perches on rising ground at the foot of which is the Grand Junction canal close to where it joins the Oxford canal. Distribution for farming produce in this area was therefore excellent.

Richard Bowers married into a wealthy local farming family, the Thorntons. His wife Elizabeth Thornton was born in 1791. The surname Thornton has lasted through successive generations of the Bowers family as a middle name; John Thornton Bowers (1832–1833), Richard Thornton Bowers (1859–1936), Thornton Richard Bowers (1895–1978), Geoffrey Thornton Bowers (1925–about 1985) and Neil Thornton Bowers (1966-present).

Whilst living at Braunston, Richard and Elizabeth Bowers had eight children, of whom two died in infancy. The seventh child, Richard Bowers, my great-great grandfather (1829 - 1895), married Eliza West (1835–1915)

Richard and Eliza lived at The Manor in nearby Brockhall and had three children, Richard Thornton (RT) Bowers (1859-1936), Rosa Jane (1862-1896) and Mary Anne (Polly or Pollie), born in 1870.

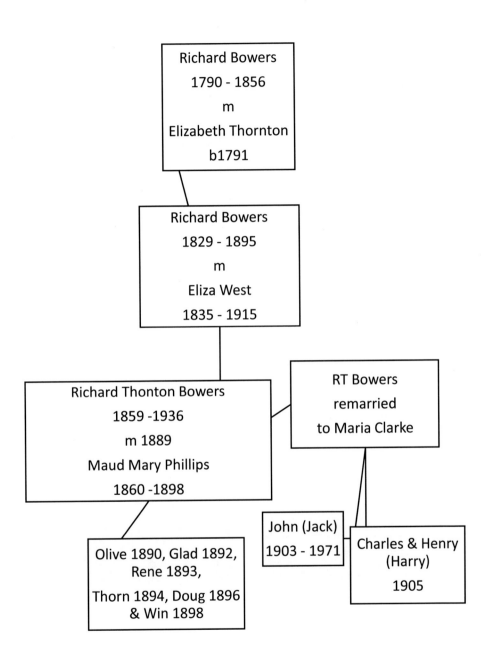

Richard Bowers
1790 - 1856
m
Elizabeth Thornton
b1791

Richard Bowers
1829 - 1895
m
Eliza West
1835 - 1915

Richard Thonton Bowers
1859 -1936
m 1889
Maud Mary Phillips
1860 -1898

RT Bowers
remarried
to Maria Clarke

Olive 1890, Glad 1892, Rene 1893,
Thorn 1894, Doug 1896 & Win 1898

John (Jack)
1903 - 1971

Charles & Henry (Harry)
1905

Brockhall Manor, 2018

Maud Mary Phillip's painting of the Manor, 1890

RT Bowers continues the line of my direct ancestors as he was my great grandfather. However, before continuing with his rather lengthy storyline, it is perhaps worth mentioning his two sisters. Polly appears from photographs to have been a very pretty girl (see photos below). In 1898, she married Herbert Clarke, an ironmonger from Towcester, at Dodford Church. Herbert Clarke's father, John, was the grocer in Long Buckby. The four bridesmaids at Polly and Herbert's Clarke's wedding were Miss Maria Clarke, Miss Ada Clarke, Olive Bowers, (later to become my paternal Grandmother) and her sister Gladys Bowers. Polly and Herbert Clarke had a daughter, Rosie, who married a man by the name of Joseph Sturgess.

Polly Bowers with her parents Richard and Eliza outside Dodford Church

Polly married Herbert Clarke in 1898

Two years later Herbert Clarke's eldest sister, Maria Clarke, the senior bridesmaid, was to become RT Bowers' second wife in 1900 after his first wife, Maud Mary died in Grendon.

The second of RT Bower's sisters, Rosa Jane, married Albert Henry Hunter of Harrow, at Brockhall Church in 1892. Rosa had been the church organist at Brockhall for ten years.

RT Bowers was born at Braunston on 30th June, 1859. On 25th September 1889, at the age of thirty, he married my great grandmother, twenty-nine-year-old Maud Mary Phillips (1860–1898), a doctor's daughter from Long Buckby. They lived at The Lower Farm in Dodford, Northamptonshire, also referred to as Dodford Lodge, and more recently as The Porch. Dodford is a hamlet

located between Weedon and Daventry, a mile north
west of Weedon station on the former main line of the
London and North Western Railway. The Grand
Junction canal and Old Roman Watling Street (A5) pass
the village. RT Bowers farmed a combined total of about
627 acres at Brockhall and Dodford, the two hamlets
being only a couple of miles apart.

Maud Mary Bowers (née Phillips) 1860 -1898

Richard Thornton Bowers 1859 - 1936

Richard Thornton and his new wife, Maud Mary Bowers wasted little time in starting their family at Dodford. My grandmother Maud Olive was the first to arrive, about ten months after the wedding, in July 1890. Olive was followed in quick succession by Gladys (July, 1892), Rosa Irene (Rene) (June, 1893), Thornton Richard (November, 1894), Douglas Phillips (September, 1896) and Winifred Evelyn (Winnie) (February, 1898).

The eldest of RTB and Maud Mary's children was my grandmother Maud (Olive) Bowers, who was born on 1st July, 1890. Olive must have had a very 'difficult' childhood, as the eldest of six young children who were to lose their mother in 1898, and then have three step brothers born to a step mother they detested.

The second of RTB's children, Glad (Gladys) married at the age thirty-one to Charles Gilman, a widowed farmer from Statfold House Tamworth.

The third daughter, Rosa Irene (Rene) married Alfred Wells from New Zealand. After the Great War they emigrated to Southern Rhodesia with their children, Ruby and Audrey. Their farm was located close to Ian Smith's family farm. Ian Smith (who became president of Rhodesia after UDI) was godfather to one of the daughters. They had emigrated with five or six other Northamptonshire families and were allocated areas of farmland by the government. Rene's younger brother Thorn Bowers had befriended Alfred in the army during the Great War. Alfred was a frequent visitor to Grendon whilst on leave, and that was there he met his future wife Rene.

The eldest son, Thornton Richard (Thorn) Bowers was born on 26th November, 1894. After war service (chapter 36) he married Grace Lomas (born 1894) of Rosehill Farm in Grendon. Grace's grandfather was a wealthy butcher in Peckham, London. After his return from the Great War, Thorn regularly drove his cattle truck down to Peckham on Mondays, picking up live cattle, sheep, pigs and lambs along the way. My father Phil Blacklee used to accompany Thorn sometimes during his school holidays. Phil remembers Lomas Butchers as 'a very substantial business.' The animals were slaughtered in an abattoir in the main street in Peckham, an event 'which attracted crowds of local children, many of whom had never seen a live bullock or pig before.' Phil remembers there was frequent 'pea soup' fog in those days due to air pollution, which made navigation difficult, but Thorn 'knew the way like the back of his hand.'

The youngest of RT and Maud Mary's children, Winifred Evelyn (Win or Winnie) Bowers, was born on 23rd February, 1898. Winnie was the final member of the Bowers family to be born at Dodford. She married Robert Sturgess from Earls Barton. It is not recorded whether Robert was related to the Joseph Sturgess who married Polly Bower's daughter Rosie. They farmed near Newark and adopted two girls, Peggy and Sue. Phil Blacklee recalls they managed to weather the financial storm in the 1920's and 'managed to keep their farm together.'

Even today, Dodford (near Weedon Northants) remains a tiny rural hamlet of about 200 inhabitants, with single track roads, no street names, no mains sewer or mains gas etc. It is however noted for the longest ford (water crossing) in the country and a Norman Grade 1 listed church, St Mary the Virgin. The vehicular access into the ford is close to Porch House where the Bowers family used to live.

In 1898, the family relocated from Dodford to Grendon, which is expanded on in chapter 31.

Maud Mary Bowers with Winnie and friend (or maid) at Porch House Dodford, shortly before the move to Grendon in 1898

Doug, Olive, Rene, Win, Glad and Thorn Bowers around the
time of the move to Grendon in 1898

Porch House in 2018

30. The Battle of Grendon

No story involving Grendon would be complete without mentioning its infamous 'battle.'

Perhaps 'battle' is an overstatement, but nevertheless the incident has relevance to this story of the farming folk of Grendon. The battle of Grendon took place only twenty years before the Bowers came to live at Grendon House Farm after the retirement of Mr JL Wright.

I must thank Eileen Wilmin and Tito Benady for describing the battle so well in their book about the village 'Grendon in Northamptonshire'. I reproduce the following story with their permission.

An explanation of the topography of the village may be helpful at this point. Grendon, or 'green hill' to give it the Anglo-Saxon meaning, does indeed sit atop a hill.

Grendon Manor House Farm (where the Longlands lived for over a century until 1920) is located at the top of the village opposite the former Crown Inn. Its farmland lies on the south-western slopes of the green hill, extending across the Nene valley towards Yardley Hastings, Castle Ashby and Whiston.

Maryland Farm House, where Wilf and Olive Blacklee lived from the early 1930s until the 1990s, is also sited at the top of the hill, with fields sloping away to the south towards Easton Maudit.

Rosehill Farm, The Lomas/Bowers' property, is half way up the northern slope of the village, three doors up from the Half Moon public house. Its farmland falls away to the east behind Chequers Lane, and northwards towards Grendon brook.

Grendon House Farm is about half a mile north of the village, on mostly flat flood plain land, beyond the brook and Blackmile Lane. Between the two lies Grendon Hall Farm, just to the south of the brook by the bridge.

In the days before mains water became available, supplies could be a problem during dry weather. When the water level in the brook fell during dry summers the tenant of Grendon House farm, John Lovell Wright, would sometimes construct a dam before the bridge by Grendon Hall. This could result in insufficient water reaching Grendon Hall farm, where the tenant was John Spencer. There was already ill feeling between the two (over a stopped-up footpath) prior to JL Wright ordering his foreman's son, Charles Ward, to dam the brook in July 1876. Wright then promptly left on holiday, perhaps wisely as it happened, leaving his men to 'hold the dam.'

Spencer's men demolished the dam the following night and Wright's men rebuilt it. This time, Wright's men laid in wait. Spencer's men spent the evening drinking in the

Half Moon public house before staggering down the hill intending to dismantle the dam on their way home. A 'dreadful riot' ensued, according to the local paper. Spencer's son Shadrack was knocked senseless, which sobered them all up a bit. Someone was sent to fetch the surgeon from Bozeat to attend to the wounded. The dam was later rebuilt under police protection. We are not told what happened afterwards, but the battle is well recorded in a lengthy poem. I will not repeat the poem here as it is far too long. It can be enjoyed in Eileen and Tito's book, or in the booklet issued by the parish council to new residents settling in the village. The bump to Shadrack's head can't have been too serious; he lived until the year 1906. He is buried next to his sister Elizabeth in Grendon churchyard, the headstones are located at the north east corner of the church.

31. The Bowers at Grendon House Farm

In chapter 29 we read how the Bowers family moved from Dodford to Grendon in the year 1898 when Win was still a toddler. RT Bowers took the tenancy of the approximately 600-acre Grendon House Farm, owned by Trinity College Cambridge, following Mr JL Wright's retirement. My Grandmother Olive told my father Phil Blacklee that having so many children so quickly and moving from a small old rectory style house into the big cold farmhouse was too much for her mother. Within months Maud Mary contracted a chill which developed into pneumonia and she died, leaving Olive and her father to bring up the younger children, 'with no doubt other help.' Maud Mary Bowers died in 1898 at the age of thirty-eight. She had written her own memorial which is perhaps worth repeating in full;

'Here lies a poor woman who always was tired

Who lived in a house where help was not hired

Her last words on Earth were 'Dear friends I am going

Where washing ain't done nor sweeping no sewing

But everything there is exact to my wishes

For where they don't eat there's no washing up dishes

I'll be where loud anthems will always be ringing

But, having no voice I'll get clear of the singing

Don't mourn for me now, don't mourn for me ever

I'm going to do nothing for ever and ever.'

MMB

There is a fine floral-patterned headstone remembering Maud Mary Bowers in Grendon churchyard located close to the Longland graves outside the porch. The high esteem in which she was held is perhaps reflected by the continued use of her maiden name throughout successive generations: Frederick Phillips Blacklee (born 1919), John Phillips Bowers (born 1923), Richard Phillips Blacklee (born 1950), and Edward Phillips Blacklee (born 1989).

Early photo of Grendon House Farm

RT Bowers with his second wife, Maria and eight of his nine
children, Grendon, 1907

32. The Aviator
Louis Bleriot, 1872–1936

RT Bower's first wife Maud Mary Phillips came from Long Buckby. Her father was the village doctor. The medical line of the Phillips family tree dates back to John, a surgeon, from Chipping Norton (born 1773).

Maud Mary Phillips had a sister, or perhaps it was a cousin, who married Arthur Cox, another doctor from Long Buckby. They were said to have been two very bright girls who befriended the young Louis Bleriot the French inventor and engineer. Bleriot developed the first effective car headlight and went on to build one of the first successful aircraft. In 1909, Bleriot became the first person to fly across the English Channel in a heavier-than-air aircraft. It was a misty day and he had no instruments. The French navy deployed a destroyer, The Escopette, into the middle of the Channel in an attempt to help him navigate. Even so, he became disoriented over 'the immense sea' for ten minutes with little view of anything other than water. He finally crash landed near Dover Castle after a flight lasting thirty-six minutes and thirty seconds, damaging the propeller and undercarriage. However, the achievement proved most profitable for Louis, as he won a £1000 prize from The Daily Mail newspaper for being the first person to cross 'La Manche' in an aeroplane.

Louis Bleriot built 900 aircraft between 1909 and the commencement of the Great War in 1914. He established flying schools at Brooklands and at Hendon Aerodrome. Bleriot landed in one of his little aeroplanes at Long Buckby one day and took the Phillips girls for a joy ride.

33. RT Bowers
1859–1936

Following on from chapter 31, Richard Thornton Bowers wasted little time finding himself a new wife after Maud Mary's death. Maud Mary Bowers had died shortly after Winnie was born in 1898 and the family's move from Dodford to Grendon. Within a couple of years, he had married grocer's daughter Maria Clarke who, like his first wife, originated from Long Buckby. 'Buckby' as it was known was a short train journey away from Grendon in those days. Castle Ashby and Earls Barton railway stations could be easily reached by bridleway and footpath from Grendon House Farm, or via the road leading up through the village.

A 1900 newspaper article describes the 'interesting wedding' at the parish church in Long Buckby; 'The church was crowded. The bride's dress was of frieze, old rose colour and trimmed with white silk and embroidered lace, with hat trimmed lace and shaded feathers. She also wore a gold and pearl bracelet, and carried a shower bouquet, both the gift of the bridegroom. The bride was given away by her father, Mr John Clarke, and the best man was her brother John Clarke Jnr. The only bridesmaid was Miss Ada Clarke (sister), who was dressed in a darker shade of frieze, also carrying a shower bouquet, and wearing a diamond ring, both gifts of the bridegroom. At 4.15, they were driven to Weedon to catch the 5.50 train to London, en-route for Brighton where the honeymoon is to be spent.'

The newspaper article is quoted in some detail as I find it intriguing that there is no record of anyone at all from Grendon attending the wedding; neither family nor friends, and the Bowers had lived at Grendon House Farm for over two years. There is a list of wedding presents recorded in the newspaper article and they are nearly all from people in Long Buckby. It would be fascinating to know what RT Bower's relatives and friends, and his six children, thought of this second marriage! Maria's future stepchildren had already ominously christened her 'the witch.' When my father Phil Blacklee dictated some family memories to Helen O'Neill (chapter 39) he had this to say about Maria:

'Now, the second wife, Maria I think her name was, was very hard and didn't like the children by the first mother. My mother Olive had a very hard time and if anything went wrong she was always blamed for the misdoings of her young brothers and sisters. This harsh upbringing persisted until mother and father (Olive and Wilf Blacklee) married in 1914.'

RT and his second wife Maria added a further three children to the family, John (Jack) Bowers (born 1903), and twins, Charles and Henry (Harry) Bowers (born 1905), bringing the total of RT Bower's children to nine.

John Reginald (Jack) Bowers was the eldest of the step brothers. He married Mary Chenells and they had two sons, Richard and David. They farmed at Lodge Farm, Easton Maudit. Farming was very difficult during the 1920s and they eventually had to give up the farm. Their eldest son Richard became a Chartered Architect and practised in Malawi. Phil Blacklee says 'he designed some good buildings as well as the airport.' Richard never married, and returned to England, to retirement in Harpole, Northamptonshire. Phil describes him as a 'delightful chap.'

The Bowers Twins Charlie & Harry b1905

Regarding the twins, Charlie died in April 1925 at the age of nineteen and was buried at Long Buckby. It must have been a very sad loss for the family, as Charlie appears to have been a very happy and mischievous child from surviving photographs. The other twin, Henry (Harry) Bowers, became a solicitor in Northampton. He absconded with client's money in 1939 shortly before the Second World War and was never heard from again (see chapter 38).

Thorn's father, RT Bowers, and step mother Maria retired from farming after Thorn returned home from fighting in France during the Great War. In April 1918 his parents purchased The Grange in Long Buckby from a Mrs Tebbitt and moved there with the thirteen-year-old twins Charlie and Harry.

The Grange, Long Buckby

In his will dated 25ᵗʰ January, 1934, RT Bowers left a life interest in The Grange, Long Buckby, together with the interest from his trust fund, to his wife Maria. The residue after Maria's death to be shared equally between all his children after bequests of £500 each to Gladys (Glad) Gilman, Rosa Irene (Rene) Wells, Winifred Eva (Win) Sturgess and Henry (Harry) Bowers, and an itemised list of personal belongings to named beneficiaries. My grandmother Maud Olive Blacklee inherited various items including a set of six Staffordshire figures and 'picture of birds in drawing-room.' These items are still in the family. The label on the back of the bird picture is inscribed 'Raphael Tuck & Sons Art Students and Amateurs Exhibition 1890 Royal Institute of Painters in Water Colours. The description of the picture is 'Siskins & ox-eye Daisies in oils.' The artist is shown as 'M Phillips Long Buckby', so the picture was presumably painted by Maud Mary Phillips my great grandmother before her marriage to RT Bowers in 1889.

Siskins and ox-eye daisies in oils

Six Staffordshire figures,
possibly by Ralph Salt 1820-1843

Under a codicil to his will RT Bowers bequeathed all his land at Grendon to his eldest son Thornton Richard Bowers. The land comprised of Fairey's land, Bett's Field and Blackmile Field.

34. Olive Bowers' Diary
1890–1990

Drawing from Olive's 1903 album

My grandmother Olive Bowers (1890–1990) attended a private junior school in Wollaston, travelling from Grendon by pony and trap. Later, she boarded in Northampton, at Castle Hall School on Abington Avenue. The former school building, located on the corner of Roe Road, now forms part of the United Reformed Church. School reports for the years 1904 and 5 show her in the first half of her classes of fourteen to seventeen-year-old girls. Thirteen-year-old Olive was given an autograph album by her auntie Alice for Christmas in 1903. This contains some lovely poems and drawings by her family and friends, giving a good insight into Olive's middle school years. Her headmistress Edith Bogle wrote the following advice in Olive's album on 14th July, 1905:

'If we look down our shoulders stoop. If our thoughts look down our character bends. It is only when we hold our heads up that the body becomes erect. It is only when our thoughts go up our life becomes erect.'

Olive kept a diary for the year 1910 (when she was about twenty) in an exercise book. This is factual rather than intimately revealing, but does give a good impression of life over a full year at Grendon House Farm. The nine Bowers children had plenty to keep them occupied before iPhones and Instagram were invented, with pets and livestock to look after, school, church, parties and concerts to attend, walks in the fields and up to Grendon, etc. Their father was kept busy with shoots in winter on his, and neighbouring, farms. Sometimes the brook flooded and Grendon became inaccessible. The house between Grendon House Farm and the village is actually called 'The Ark'. In springtime, the lambs are born and the family enjoyed lamb's tails for dinner. There were regular trips to market to buy or sell horses, cattle and sheep. Castle Ashby and Earls Barton railway station was only a short walk away by bridleway and footpath, although the family often used a pony and trap, or bicycle, to reach the station by the road up through the village.

Olive and her sisters spent a lot of their time 'washing and spring cleaning, churning and soaking'. They made pies, lard and butter for selling in local villages. Eggs were fetched almost daily from nearby Whiston village to sell with their own. I speculate that this might have been from their friend William Pell Mackaness' Manor Farm at Whiston.

In summer months, Olive Bowers' churning had to be done early in the morning or the butter wouldn't set. The large quantities of produce are illustrated by her 1910 diary entry stating that the girls took 44lbs of butter to Wollaston by pony and trap on 24th June.

It wasn't all work and no play however; there were regular parties, dances and concerts to attend. On 29th October, Olive went to London by train to buy a coat, and to see the new German operetta, *The Chocolate Soldier.* On 31st October, she went to the cinematograph (possibly in Wellingborough – she doesn't say where) to see *Uncle Jones Cabin.* Both productions were notable in their day.

Regal cinema Wellingborough before demolition

On Friday 31st June 1910, Olive's birthday, she received 'lots of presents.' The following day she 'saw W in the evening, brought four cows.' This presumably refers to Wilf Blacklee of Grendon Manor Farm to whom she was married four years later.

35. The Grendon Grand National winner

Grendon Hall, 2018

Maybe my grandmother Olive Blacklee's home-churned butter (chapter 34) played a vital part in winning the Grand National in 1901! The winning mount, Gruden, was owned, bred and trained by Bernard Bletsoe of Hall Farm, Grendon.

It was snowing at Aintree that day and Bletsoe had the bright idea of packing butter in the horse's hooves. The ploy worked so well that jockey Arthur Nightingale had an easy 'hack' around the course chatting to other jockeys until nearing the finish when he left the other riders behind with the immortal words, 'well I must be going now, so ta-ta.'

Arthur Nightingale (1868–1944) rode in fifteen Grand Nationals, riding three winners. The snow was so deep in 1901 the race was in doubt. Only five of the original twenty-four starters finished.

Bernard Bletsoe also trained Rubio, but not at the time of that horse's National win in 1908 when ridden by his son Henry. Rubio was put to pulling a hotel bus in Towcester to strengthen his legs before the race. Bernard later took the Elms Stud in Denton where Richard Bowers later ran his successful stables for many years. Richard Bowers had one of Gruden's shoes in a mounted display case on the wall at the Elms. He left it there when he retired to Grendon, but recent enquiries reveal it has been mislaid by the new occupiers!

36. The Bowers during the Great War

At the commencement of the Great War of 1914-1918, Thorn Bowers, together with Bert Taylor (a Grendon Thatcher) had joined the Yeomanry together. They rode their own horses to France. Fortunately, both men survived, Thorn actually returned with the same chestnut mare had taken to war. Thorn wasn't unscathed however, for he had been badly gassed in the trenches in France. The fate of Bert's horse is not recorded.

There was an interesting report on the invisible menace of German poison gas in the Daily Telegraph on 20th March, 1918:

'Our men work, sleep, and eat with their gas-masks handy, no further away than their left hips, and practise wearing these things on and off duty, marching, running, and riding. These practices produce uncanny scenes along the roads and in the fields of war, so inhuman and fantastic, that if any creature came from another planet and visited this Western front, and fell among a group of these masked men, busy with mysterious labour, above earth dwellings dug into hillsides or among the ruins of churches, mediaeval mansions, and farmsteads, smashed to matchwood he would be terrified by the beastlike aspect of the earth's inhabitants, and believe that they were evil monsters who had entered into possession of man's inheritance after the destruction of his civilisation.'

The effects of poison gas, together with his asthma, meant Thorn had difficulty breathing for the rest of his life. He died in 1978 at the age of eighty-four.

Bert Taylor became an important figure at the Borough of Wellingborough, including Mayor for a while. Unfortunately, Thorn and Bert fell out later in life over a land deal. Bert had persuaded Thorn to sell him a sizeable strip of farm land, supposedly for a retirement bungalow. Bert upset Thorn by applying for planning permission for several houses.

Thorn's younger brother Douglas Phillips Bowers joined the South Staffordshire regiment as a private in the Great War. He was killed in France on 15th October, 1915 shortly before his twentieth birthday. Doug is buried at Croques Military Cemetery near Bethune, Pas de Calais. I have visited his grave which is beautifully kept and quite easily accessible from Calais. My grandmother Olive Blacklee (his elder sister) was Doug's executor who received his three campaign medals and brass memorial plaque commonly known as the 'Death

Penny.' The medals are the 1914 Star (Mons Star), the British War Medal and the Victory Medal awarded to servicemen who had served from 1914 or 1915. The three are affectionately known together as 'Pip, Squeak and Wilfred' after a popular comic strip in the Daily Mirror which coincided with their issue in the 1920s. The 'Death Penny' was issued to next of kin of all personnel killed as a result of the War. Douglas Bowers is remembered on Great War memorials both inside and outside Grendon Church.

Bert Taylor.   Oliver Taylor.

Bert and Oliver Taylor

WWI Memorial plaque - the 'death penny'

Douglas Phillips Bowers

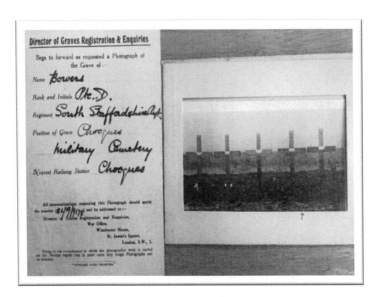

Official notification of Douglas Bowers' grave
location in Pas de Calais

Douglas Bowers with death penny and medals

37. The Bowers after the Great War

Thorn Bowers returned home from fighting in France at the end of the war in 1918. He took over the tenancy of Grendon House Farm from his father and married Grace Lomas shortly afterwards. The first four of their children were born at the Farm; Douglas (born 1920), Rob (born 1922), John (born 1923) and Geoff (born 1925). Due to the dire farming conditions during post war years around the 1920s, the tenancy of Grendon House Farm was relinquished. Fortunately, Grace's family still owned Rosehill Farm in Grendon. This comprised a pretty stone and tiled detached house with farm buildings and about eighty acres. It was rented out to an army major at the time. (This may have been the Major Brinton whose family lodged at Maryland Farm during the Second World War. Olive was particularly close to the Major's daughter Julie Brinton who stayed in touch with the family until Olive's death in 1990). Grace (née Lomas) purchased Rosehill Farm from her Grandmother Spencer, and, after serving notice to rehouse the Major, the Bowers moved in. At the time, the Bowers family consisted of Thorn and Grace and their children Douglas, Robert, John and Geoff. Richard (born 1931) and Ann (born 1933) were born after the move to Rosehill. Ann still lives there and has a letter from a property valuer who described the condition of the property as 'very run down' at the time of the move. Fortunately, Thorn was able to sell one of the bottom fields beyond the brook to help out with the family's finances. This field is now part of Grendon House Farm.

Thornton Richard Bowers

38. The Crooked Solicitor
Harry Bowers

My father Phil Blacklee remembers Thorn Bowers' step brother Harry Bowers as a 'nice man' who would sometimes take him to lunch at the Cheyne Walk club before the Second World War. This was whilst Phil was working at Howards Quantity Surveyors. His uncle Harry was a solicitor with an office in Wood Street, Northampton.

Harry had a secret life as a gambler and the temptation to dip into his office client's account became too much for him to resist. He misappropriated client's money and was caught. An article in the Mercury & Herald of Friday March 21st, 1941 explains the circumstances, under the heading:

'NORTHAMPTON SOLICITOR STRUCK OFF'

'The Disciplinary Committee constituted under the Solicitors' Act (1932) sitting in public at Carey Street London WC, ordered the name of Henry Bowers, formerly of 3 Wood Street Northampton, and of Long

Buckby, to be struck off the roll for professional misconduct.

The Committee found that the allegation made against him – that he misappropriated £150, part of a sum of £211 14s. 8d. received by him for investment on behalf of a client, Mrs Kate Selina Sabbage – had been substantiated'.

Harry Bowers vanished after that incident and the family never heard from him again.

It is strange the way history sometimes repeats itself. In the 1980/90s, I regularly met a local solicitor, Adrian Jackman, together with his adorable wife who was also a solicitor, and their colleagues, for lunch at the Cheyne Walk Club. Like my father before with Harry, I too considered Adrian Jackman a 'nice man.' He was president of Northampton Law Society and a Freeman of the City of London.

Jackman was caught stealing from his office client's account, to the tune of almost £2m. He was struck off by the Law Society in 2003 and sent to prison. He 'wove a labyrinthine web of dishonesty by inventing clients, making false wills and using bogus paperwork to obtain loans from High Street banks.' The chairman of the Solicitors Disciplinary Tribunal announcing the decision, said

'This is one of the most appalling cases we've heard.' Jackman had been sending £1,000 a month to a mistress in South Africa.

Harry Bowers - 1917

39. The occupational therapist
Helen O'Neill 1952 - 2016

My first cousin Helen Margaret O'Neill (née Smith) was keenly interested in family history. She was entrusted with any important papers, photographs or other records. If anyone wanted to know anything about the family they would ask Helen.

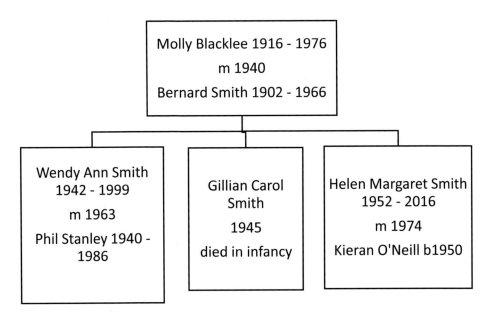

Molly Blacklee 1916 - 1976

m 1940

Bernard Smith 1902 - 1966

Wendy Ann Smith 1942 - 1999

m 1963

Phil Stanley 1940 - 1986

Gillian Carol Smith

1945

died in infancy

Helen Margaret Smith 1952 - 2016

m 1974

Kieran O'Neill b1950

On 30th April, 1940 Molly Blacklee, aged twenty-four, (my father Phil's older sister), married thirty-eight-year-old Bernard Smith of Home Farm, Little Oakley. The service was held at St Mary's Church in Grendon with the reception afterwards at the bride's parents' Maryland Farm. Bernard Smith was born to Henry, thirty-nine, a farmer, and Martha, thirty-three, a domestic servant.

Molly and Bernard Smith had three daughters whilst living with Bernard's parents at Home Farm: Wendy Anne, Gillian Carol (died in infancy), and Helen Margaret (later to become Mrs Helen O'Neill who spent countless hours spent researching our family history).

Times were very hard for the young family at the run-down antiquated farm near Corby. In 1954 or 5, when my grandfather Wilf Blacklee was ailing (he died in 1958), Molly and Bernard (together with their daughters Wendy and Helen) moved to Grendon. The farm inventory for their final year at Home Farm comprised one horse, thirty-three cattle, three pigs and 182 poultry. Bernard took a formal tenancy of Maryland Farm from Wilf and Olive Blacklee in 1955 (the lease on Home Farm, Little Oakley from landlords The Boughton Estates Ltd ended 25th March 1955, after five generations of Smith tenants). The Smith name thereafter disappears from the family tree as there were no sons in either Bernard or his brother Alec's families.

Maryland Farm was a far cry from the prestigious Grendon Manor Farm where Wilf Blacklee was raised by the Longlands. The 1956 inventory of Maryland Farm comprised one horse, thirty-eight cattle, one pig and 182 poultry. By 1959, there were twenty-three pigs and 500 head of poultry.

Fordson N type tractor at Maryland Farm
(girl and cat not identified)

Helen with her pet cow Susan in 1958

Helen's father Bernard Smith would take his old tractor and trailer down the hill to Grendon Primary School after lunch to collect the kitchen slops for his pigs. This was the Fordson Model N (produced between 1929–1945) seen in the photo. Jonathan Sayles of Grendon who was a pupil at the time remembers Bernard had a farm labourer 'who always wore a brown smock.'

Helen Smith with her grandmother Olive Blacklee at
Maryland Farm, Grendon, Friday 26th February, 1960

Helen Smith with her parents Molly and Bernard in Grendon

Helen at Maryland Farm in 1965

Helen Smith was a very bright girl who shared her Grandmother Olive's love for art, cooking, people and animals. In April 1965 she won the first prize of £10 in the Mercury & Herald Egg Week painting competition judged by Mr T Osborne Robinson, the artist and scenic designer at Northampton Repertory Theatre. Olive and Helen displayed similar qualities of calmness, kindness and natural leadership. Olive was the eldest of the Bowers' nine siblings. Helen was head girl of Wollaston secondary school before embarking on a career as an Occupational Therapist. After leaving school, she attended the Northampton 'ladies finishing school,'

Priory College, the St Andrew's School of Occupational Therapy. She excelled in her profession and in 1980, after attending a course in America, had a book published about managing anger which, together with a second edition, became text books within the profession. I have recently seen a copy of the original book advertised for £62.95 in paperback form on Amazon!

Maryland Farm Grendon in the 1950s

In 1974, Helen married Kieran O'Neill at St Mary's Church, Grendon, with the reception in the village hall. They have two sons. In November 1978 she was appointed Head Occupational Therapist at St Andrew's

Hospital Northampton. Helen retired due to illness in 2013.

The first symptoms of Helen's dreadful Motor Neurone disease became apparent after she suffered a fall in Northampton. She stoically fought the illness for several years before finally succumbing on 23rd June 2016. Helen was laid to rest at Olney Green Burial Ground on 7th July 2016 after a well-attended humanist service.

40. The Highwayman
William Bowers 1731-1787

In these closing chapters I should like to tell you more about the highwayman William Bowers, a leading member of the notorious Culworth Gang, who was introduced in the opening story. I have no idea whether I am actually related to him as, even though the family tree for my branch of the Bowers family dates back to 1720, William's name doesn't appear. My cousin Helen (chapter 39) was convinced from her extensive research that he was related and that is good enough for me. Certainly, the area in which William Bowers lived and operated from was very close to the villages in Northamptonshire where our direct Bowers forebears lived at around that time.

In the latter part of the 18th century, the village of Culworth in South Northants was home to a bunch of individuals involved in poaching, housebreaking and highway robbery. Culworth was ideally placed for such activities. There were two ancient drove tracks through the village, useful for making a quick escape. A nearby turnpike through Whittlebury forest was used by coaches and goods carts travelling between Oxford and Northampton. Whittlebury Forest had also been the occasional haunt of the famous highwayman Dick Turpin (1705–1739) fifty years before. Turpin reputedly had a narrow escape from the Bow Street Runners at the Green Man Inn, Syresham. He escaped into the forest on foot but his saddled horse Black Bess was captured by the Constables.

The Culworth Gang consisted of up to fifteen members. They were mostly casual farm labourers who would have struggled to find any agricultural work during the winter months. At least two of them were educated men. William Abbott was the parish clerk of Sulgrave (and hid his share of the loot in the church!) Gilkes was from a good local family and went along for the excitement. When the Constables finally closed in on the gang, Gilkes quickly emigrated to the West Indies where he made a fortune on a plantation. The Culworth gang dressed in smock frocks and masks and, like Dick Turpin, they blackened their faces for disguise. Clearly, highwaymen had little respect for the law as the blackening or disguise of faces whilst in a forest was prohibited in 1723 under The Black Act.

The Culworth Gang's preparations for attack were meticulous. Their behaviour was firm but not brutal by the standards of the day. They were unarmed apart from billy clubs and they never killed anyone. They didn't attack a drove of animals as drovers carried flintlock firearms and were guarded by 'heavies' who were often fugitives from justice themselves. Although many people must have been aware of their identities, no one was willing to stand against the Culworth Gang due to fear of forceful reprisals. The ringleaders including William Bowers were eventually betrayed by two members of the gang Richard Law and William Pettifer who were arrested at a hostelry in Towcester. A suspicious landlord discovered smocks and masks in their bags after they had drunk too much and decided to stay the night. The landlord summoned the Constable and the gang were rounded up. The betrayal didn't save Law and Pettifer though, they were also condemned to death together with the ringleaders.

The Culworth Gang caused general mayhem in the Midlands for around twenty years and their story is immortalised in a song by Fairport Convention, and others, called 'Close to the Wind.' The words of the song explain that the robberies committed by the Gang were to keep their families from starving. Also that following their arrest the Gang members left fifty children around Culworth without fathers!

41. The Hangings

The seven members of the Culworth Gang committed for trial at Northamptonshire Summer Assizes in 1787 were: William Bowers, three members of the Smith family (John the elder who was leader of the gang, and his sons John and William), Richard Law, William Pettifer and William Tyrrel. William Bowers had had a 'chance child' by Elizabeth Tyrrel in 1785 and she was also tried, on the charge of receiving stolen goods.

The list of charges against the gang members was extensive. It included robbery of the Banbury carrier Frederick Richardson and the Mercury newsman

William Cotton who are mentioned in the opening story. Richardson was ambushed at Sturdy's Castle near Blenheim Palace, and Cotton on Banbury Lane drover's track at the bottom of Hunsbury Hill in Northampton.

Bowers was said to be the most obstinate and hardened criminal of the lot in court, swearing and cursing loudly throughout his trial. He was convicted of stealing a variety of items including fifteen shillings, clothes and meat. He shouted out in court 'a man had no more chance here than a cat in hell without claws.' Five of the accused were given the death sentence; one who turned against the others was transported to Australia. Tyrell and the younger Smiths received lesser sentences. The public execution of Bowers, Smith Snr, Law and Pettifer took place at midday on Friday, August 4th on Northampton Heath (nowadays called The Racecourse), close to the White Elephant public house. The execution was watched by a crowd approaching 5,000 people. As the entire population of Northampton stood at about 7,000 towards the end of the 18th century, it shows the huge popularity of public 'swing offs,' as such hangings were popularly known.

The prisoners were conveyed to the gallows on a couple of horse drawn carts. They stopped off at the Bantam Cock (in Abington Square) in accordance with tradition for one final drink. In the 18th century the Bantam Cock was the edge of the built-up area of the town.

The prisoners were forced to stand up on the back of the cart and the hangman's noose was fitted around their necks. At an agreed signal the horse was driven forward, and with any luck, the resultant tightening of the ligature and height of the drop would snap the condemned person's neck. This method might sound cruel to us today, but it was a definite improvement on Dick Turpin's short drop hanging and resultant slow strangulation in York in 1739. It is not recorded what happened to William Bower's body after it was cut down, other than the report that no one came to collect it. The mother of his child, Elizabeth Tyrrel, was presumable in custody herself. Bowers was most likely buried in a convenient spot nearby by the prison staff. Hopefully he was left to rest in peace unlike Dick Turpin forty-six years earlier whose body was immediately dug up by body snatchers intent on stealing cadavers for medical research.

I like to think the newsman William Cotton got his revenge by selling published copies of the gang's confessions, which contained details of forty-seven different crimes, of which thirty were committed in Northamptonshire. The published confessions were sold in several formats, from a double-sided broadsheet to a six-penny booklet.

In chapter 8 about Boughton Green Fair I touched upon the story of 'Captain Slash.' I will conclude with brief details of this unsavoury character who also 'died with his boots on' (another popular euphuism for hanging) at

Northampton in 1826. George Catherall's alias 'Captain Slash' was a Pugilist, a bare-knuckle fighter, who 'graced the Fair with his presence' in 1826. His nickname came from the distinctive scarring from a fractured skull usually covered by silk cloth. Catherall was leader of a large gang reportedly numbering up to ninety strong, who preyed on booth holders and showmen alike at midnight when the Fairman's coffers were bulging with takings. The attack on the menagerie ticket office was thwarted by the quick-witted lion trainer who fetched out a huge, scary, but quite tame beast. This deterred the attackers from disturbing the animals, but the poor keeper was severely beaten for his troubles and was later found in a cellar succumbed from his injuries. Catherall was eventually arrested after a twenty-minute free-for-all fight which resulted in him breaking his wrist and a couple of ribs. He was charged at Northampton Assizes with a token case of assault and robbery. The judge observed that as this comprised Highway Robbery in his opinion, and as the accused was clearly guilty, the sentence was death by hanging. Catherall suffered the same early form of short drop hanging as Dick Turpin, resulting in his body twitching and convulsing for quite two minutes before it stilled. Further humiliation followed with scores of women rushing up to the gallows out of the enormous crowd after he had been 'turned off' to rub the dead man's hand on their warts, a superstition known as 'rubbing wens.'

George Catherall had always promised his mother he would not 'die with his boots on.' The story goes that just before the 'swing off' whilst Catherall was having the noose adjusted around his neck, shortly before his cap was drawn over his face, he prised off his boots and kicked them into the crowd. A Northampton man who caught one boot was able to purchase the other for 2s 6d the following day in Northampton Market Place to complete the pair.

43. Conclusion

When I started researching the family history, I had never even heard of two of my great grandmothers on my maternal side, Adelheid Franziska Kauffman (chapter 16) and Martha Williams (chapter 15). I knew very little about the other two, Annie Longland (chapter 3) and Maud Mary Phillips (chapter 31). I had heard a little about the Gimsons from my mother and now I have been intrigued to learn so much more. Inevitably, I wish I had shown interest years ago when there were more of the older generation around to ask, but at least I feel I have been able to safeguard some of my cousin Helen O'Neill's noble efforts on family research for posterity.

The following family trees show my relationship to each of my great grandmothers.

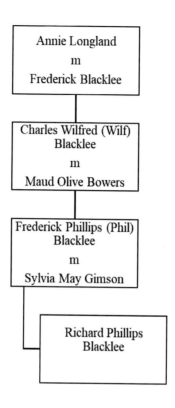

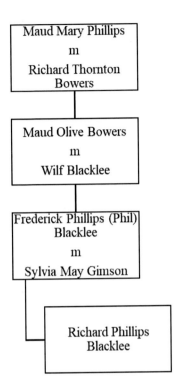

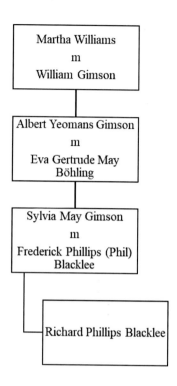

Martha Williams
m
William Gimson

Albert Yeomans Gimson
m
Eva Gertrude May
Böhling

Sylvia May Gimson
m
Frederick Phillips (Phil)
Blacklee

Richard Phillips Blacklee

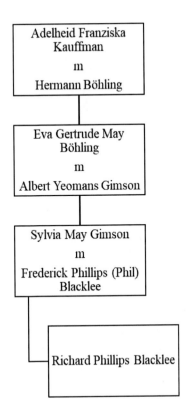

Acknowledgements

Grateful thanks are due to my cousin Helen O'Neill for displaying such a keen interest in her side of the family, collating records and preparing invaluable family trees. Helen's mother Molly Smith was my father's sister. Thanks also to my father Phil, and my favourite 'auntie' Ann of Rosehill Farm, for their recollections of the old days, to Kieran, Will & Joe O'Neill, and Curley Corbett, for loaning me Helen's documents, without which have I would not have undertaken this project.

To Jon Sayles, Eileen Wilmin and Margaret Liddle for help on matters concerning Grendon, to Elaine Winter née Bailey for her assistance with the sections about Yardley Hastings, Whiston and Brafield-on-the Green, to the author Neil Wooler for his general encouragement and advice and invaluable knowledge of the days of the local railways, to Dr Malcolm Blacklee and Dr James Dodson for their contributions. Special thanks to Neil and Glyn Hatfield the Gimson family historians, for their information about my mother's side of the family which has been quite an eye opener for me.

Thanks to the author Morgen Bailey for guiding me in the direction of Caroline and Andy of 3P Publishing, and to Andy of 3P for showing me how to turn an incomprehensible draft into something hopefully approaching a readable book.

And finally, to my lovely wife Carolyn and my family for putting up with my preoccupation over the past few months, and constant questions about spelling!

Bibliography:

Tito Benady & Eileen Wilmin, Grendon in Northamptonshire, Gibraltar Books Ltd 1994

Eric Tonks, The Ironstone Quarries of the Midlands, Book Law Publications 2009

About the author:

After a successful career as a Chartered Surveyor and Arbitrator newly retired Richard Blacklee was given his cousin Helen's family research papers after her untimely death.

Believing the fascinating history would probably be lost for ever unless he did something about it, Richard began his second career as a writer. His interviews with senior members of the family and extensive further research revealed some incredible stories of life, death and survival that form the heart of this book.

Carpe diem! quam minimum credula postero.

'When you cease to enquire, stupidity has you in its grasp.'

Richard lives in Grendon, Northamptonshire with his wife Carolyn. They have three sons and at the time of writing, have become grandparents for the first time.